AMERICAN BRILLIANT CUT GLASS

ALSO BY LOUISE BOGGESS:

Fiction Techniques That Sell
Writing Articles That Sell
Journey to Citizenship
Writing Fillers That Sell
Your Social Security Benefits

AMERICAN BRILLIANT CUT GLASS

by
Bill and Louise Boggess

CROWN PUBLISHERS, INC., NEW YORK

To our mothers
Ruth M. Boggess
Hattie M. Bradford

Inquiries should be addressed to Crown Publishers, Inc., One Park Avenue,
New York, N.Y. 10016

Printed in the United States of America

Published simultaneously in Canada by General Publishing Company Limited.

Designed by Manuela Paul

Library of Congress Cataloging in Publication Data

Boggess, Bill.
    American brilliant cut glass.

    Includes index.
    1. Cut glass, American.   I.   Boggess, Louise, joint
author.   II.   Title.
NK5203.B63   1976   748.2'913   76-14479
ISBN 0-517-52525-9

Fourth Printing, June, 1979

CONTENTS

Acknowledgments   vi
Preface   vii
1. Crystal Gazing   1
2. Artistry on Glass   10
3. Identification by Motif   19
4. Identification by Pattern   36
5. Identification by Signature   85
6. The Buying Game   109
7. Evaluating Cut Glass   129
8. Helpful Tips for the Collector   153

Appendix

SIGNATURES   173
INDEX OF ILLUSTRATED PATTERNS   176

Index   180

Acknowledgments

WE WISH TO ACKNOWLEDGE THE ASSISTANCE AND ENCOURAGEMENT OF many helpful people in researching and compiling this book.

Glen DeYoe gave us the benefit of his professional experience in photography and served as our chief adviser in this field.

The following collectors and dealers permitted us to photograph their collections for illustrations in the book: Irma Adams, Mr. and Mrs. Harry Aubright, Helen Breeding, Roy Brown, Argie Burwell, E. E. Bustamente, Don Carr, George Clark, Patrick Curry, Helen D'Arcy, Barbara W. Doble, Ann Dunlap, Lucinda Baker Griener, Adolph F. Hansen, Beth Hazlett, the Hebels, Marie H. Hegarty, Evelyn Henzi, Dorothy Herrington, Dr. and Mrs. G. R. Hunt, Rita Klyce, Madeline Lundin, Myra Matas, C. W. Moody, Dottie Murphy, Tom and Theresa O'Connell, Mrs. A. L. Moreggia, Doris Patterson, Mrs. Jack Pelzner, Alice Peri, Thelma Prouse, Mildred Quinn, Jean Rieth, David Seiling, Ardene Fairchild Smith, Sharalyn Spiteri, Mr. and Mrs. Alexander Tisnado, Mr. and Mrs. Jack Walker, and Henrietta Wise.

Several hundred dealers—far too many to list—freely shared their knowledge and experience. Miss Lucille Egginton added information about her father. E. R. Schweizer helped with the research on American colored-cut-to-clear glass. Craig Slifer and Lucille Hackett sketched a number of the signatures.

William L. Wixson, Otis Gerould, and Jerry Kusak shared their experiences as old-time cutters during the Brilliant Period. Our favorite repairman, Scotty, showed that damaged pieces can be restored to beauty.

Editors Frank Knight, Lillian Potter, Don Brown, William J. Croker, John F. Malone, Don Henry, Charlotte Prentice, and Gray D. Boone published our articles and furthered our research by forwarding letters from the readers. Many readers generously shared their knowledge.

Kitty and Russell Umbraco, 6019 Arlington Boulevard, Richmond, California, permitted us to reprint pages from the Averbeck, Bergen, and Pitkin and Brooks catalogs. Carl U. Fauster, P.O. Box 7413, Toledo, Ohio, gave us permission to reprint a page from the 1896 Libbey Catalog. The First California Regional Group of National Early American Glass Club let us reprint pages from a Hawkes booklet.

Museums and historical societies gave assistance, too. Without the vital assistance of the Toledo Museum of Art we could not have identified so many Libbey patterns.

To all those who helped, we acknowledge a deep debt of gratitude.

Preface

A SMALL INHERITANCE OF CUT GLASS STIMULATED OUR INTEREST IN IT. Through this interest we have collected a good deal of information that we believe will help collectors identify and appreciate cut glass more, whether they have a few pieces or many.

We began the research on this book by studying the published books and magazine articles on cut glass. As we gathered new information, we began to write for national antiques magazines, and readers of our articles generously volunteered additional facts.

Covering antique shows for these magazines opened the door for us to interview over three hundred dealers who buy and sell cut glass. These dealers called our attention to new signatures, places to locate signatures, and the names of specific patterns. To help us name other patterns we acquired old catalog reprints, and these led the way to museums and the information they offered on cut glass.

Through these and other contacts we located several old cutters and interviewed them. They added a wealth of firsthand information.

Finally, as we became more and more knowledgeable, we spoke to women's clubs on cut glass and had the members bring in pieces for identification. This resulted in a television series on antique glass and instructing a college class on the subject. All these things not only increased our knowledge of cut glass but introduced us to many collectors who shared their experiences with us.

Fortunately, we also made several trips to Europe, where we visited factories and watched the cutting of modern pieces like those now being imported. In our own country we visited the Kusak Cut Glass Company, which still cuts and engraves fine glass. And as we came upon more and more glass from Canada, we researched the available material on old Canadian cut glass as well.

Every item pictured in this book except one belongs to collectors or dealers. Most have been acquired recently or inherited.

We have endeavored to put all the information we collected from all the above sources in a practical book to guide the collector, the dealer, and the appraiser in the identification and evaluation of American cut glass of the Brilliant Period.

BILL AND LOUISE BOGGESS

A thing of beauty is a joy for ever:
Its loveliness increases . . .

From *Endymion* by Keats

1.
CRYSTAL GAZING

MANY OF YOU PROBABLY OWN ONE OR MORE PIECES OF AMERICAN CUT glass that you inherited, bought, or received as a gift. In the forty years of its production, brilliant cut glass ranked as first choice for a wedding, anniversary, or birthday present.

Most families so highly valued "the cut glass" that they used it only for "company" dinners or special occasions; and, moreover, a cut glass bowl brimming with chopped fruit or a nappy filled with homemade strawberry preserves could turn any average meal into a "company" dinner. Remember how carefully your mother or grandmother washed her cut glass following such a feast? Then she would painstakingly return the tumblers, bowls, or cruets to the glass china closet to await the next special occasion.

The national bicentennial of 1976 coincided with the one hundredth birthday of brilliant cut glass. By attaining this age, it technically assumes its rightful place as an antique. Although Americans did cut glass before 1876, they used simple designs reminiscent of the English and Irish flutes, diamonds, and fans.

The 1876 Centennial Exposition in Philadelphia introduced a brilliantly cut glass that expressed American originality and individuality. At that exposition attention was focused on the elegance and beauty of American cut glass by means of exhibits by outstanding glass companies. Exhibitors included—to name just a few—the New England Glass Company (later Libbey Glass Company); Mt. Washington Glass Company (later Pairpoint Corporation); J. D. Dobelmann; Hobbs, Brockunier Company; Gillinder & Sons; and C. Dorflinger & Sons.

Dorflinger displayed a cut and engraved wine set. The engraved panels of the bottle pictured the Goddess of Liberty, the United States coat of arms, and the city of Philadelphia. The seals of the thirty-eight states appeared on the

2 wineglasses. William Gillinder set up a complete glassworks to show the entire process, from the molten glass to the cutting of souvenir pieces that were sold to exhibition visitors. Despite this dramatic demonstration at the exposition, however, the general public and especially the wealthy still considered imported glass superior to American-made.

During the 1890s a number of wholesale and retail dealers continued to sell American cut glass as cut glass imported from England or the Continent, in the belief that the consumer preferred the imported product. Since Christian Dorflinger had brought skilled artisans over from England and the Continent, the glass produced in his factory closely resembled its European counterparts. Dorflinger's son, William, reported that some unscrupulous dealers and wholesalers shipped the company's glass to Europe and brought it back as "imported," to get a higher price.

In 1893, to combat such gross misrepresentation, American glass manufacturers began an extensive advertising campaign to make the public aware of "American rich cut glass" and to distinguish it from the inferior type coming from Europe. A number of firms added the word "rich" to the company name and placed it on their catalogs, among them Bergen Rich Cut Glass and Wright Rich Cut Glass.

Meanwhile, the leaders in the glass industry achieved international recognition through exhibits at worldwide expositions. In 1889, T. G. Hawkes and Company won the Grand Prize at the Paris Exposition for their Grecian and Chrysanthemum patterns (Ill. 1). At the World's Columbian Exposition in Chicago in 1893, the Libbey Glass Company erected a large factory where craftsmen made and cut glass. The Crystal Art Room of the Libbey exhibit displayed cut glass in a setting of mirrors and spun-glass draperies (Ill. 2). At this same exposition, J. Hoare & Company won a gold medal for its exhibit.

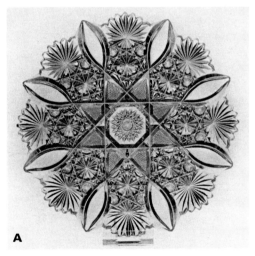

1A. A 7-inch plate in Grecian pattern by Hawkes, patented October 25, 1887. **B.** A copy of the Grand Prize Certificate awarded Hawkes at the Paris Exposition in 1889 for Grecian and Chrysanthemum patterns. *First Regional Group National Early American Glass Club.* **C.** Five-inch nappy in Chrysanthemum pattern, patented November 4, 1890. *Shaun Miller*

A

C

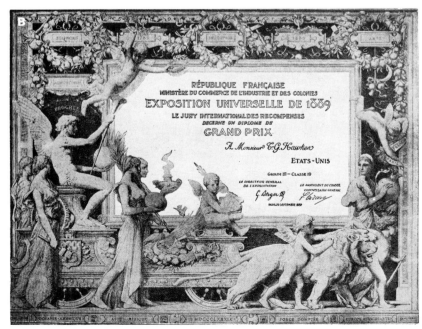

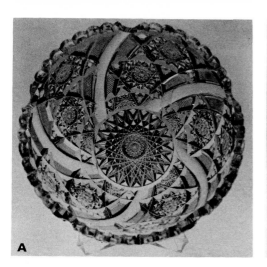

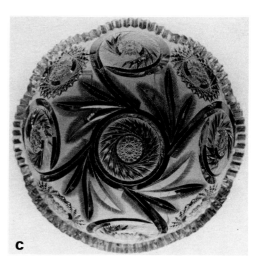

2. Three 8-inch berry bowls that illustrate the rhythmic cutting found in designs of the Brilliant Period after 1900. **A.** Chain of hobstars and triple bands radiate from a hobstar center; signed Egginton. *Eleanor Lovett.* **B.** Curved miters frame pinwheels to produce a rhythmic design; signed Clark. **C.** Curved miters with blaze flow from a circled pinwheel. *Madeline Lundin*

Even in its heyday, cut glass commanded such a high price that only the carriage trade, the White House, or the heads of foreign governments could afford to buy complete dinner services or to decorate their homes extensively with it. Within a span of forty years, President Porforio Diaz of Mexico, the Crown Prince of Sweden, and Chiang Kai-shek purchased complete dinner services from the Hawkes firm, which gave the name "Brazilian" to that cut for President Diaz.

The Prince of Wales, later King Edward VIII, ordered a set of fluted glassware from Dorflinger for use on his private train when he toured Canada and the United States. President Mario Menocal of Cuba bought 2,300 pieces of glass engraved with a coat of arms from Dorflinger. Such examples represent only a few of the outstanding foreign purchases.

With the outbreak of World War I, the production of cut glass slowed down greatly because the government needed lead, the essential ingredient of this prismatic glass, for the war effort. Unable to get the necessary materials, many companies went out of business. After the war, the few factories that had managed to continue in business turned their attention to producing a less costly glass (Ill. 3).

3. Two tall compotes that show the contrast between high, brilliant cutting and the cutting of the Flower Period. **A.** This 10-inch compote in flashed stars and hobstars has a hobstar base. **B.** An 8-inch compote with a fluted stem and single star base; flowers dominate the bowl. *Jean Rieth*

4   Within recent years, interest in antiques has stimulated the collecting of this prewar glass of such rare beauty. Perhaps this spirit has inspired you to start a collection or add new pieces to your present collection. Regardless of what stimulated your interest, you doubtless want to learn more about what you already own and perhaps also how to choose additional pieces of this Brilliant Period cut glass. We warn you: the more you learn, the more you will want to know.

Periods of Cut Glass

American cut glass production can be divided into three periods: Early, Brilliant, and Flower. All three exhibit distinctive characteristics as to patterns, types of pieces, and composition of glass. During the Early Period (circa 1830-76) most of the cutters had immigrated from Europe, and so they imitated the shallow cuts and simple patterns of England, Ireland, and the Continent. A pattern might consist entirely of flat flutes or a row of thumbprints. Etching and engraving rather than cutting characterized much of this early glass. In mid-century, glass companies favored heavier-cut patterns, such as ovals of pointed diamonds or groupings of crosshatched squares (English strawberry diamond) with fan borders.

Most of the early cutting shops specialized in making shades and globes for oil lamps, but a few, such as B. Bakewell & Company and John L. Gilliland & Company, made tableware. Since the factories followed the European formula for making glass, pieces of this period have a slight grayish tint.

Because of the Civil War's demand for materials and manpower, many glass companies went out of business at that time or turned to making pressed glass. A few, such as J. Hoare & Company and C. Dorflinger & Sons, not only weathered the war but met the strong competition of pressed glass, to become outstanding producers in the Brilliant Period.

For the next thirty years, American cut glass of the Brilliant Period (1876-1906) monopolized the national and international market because of the unusual clarity of the lead glass and the originality of the designs. In this period the craftsman cut most of the surface of the glass to produce a prismatic sparkle, thereby suggesting the name "brilliant." To achieve this brilliance, American cutters greatly refined and elaborated the designs of the Irish, English, and Bohemians, and at the beginning of the period, they often combined two different designs to create a pattern of overall cutting, as in the case of the Russian Pattern (Ill. 4).

At the height of the Brilliant Period, the master craftsman might combine several geometric figures in an ornate, highly individualized pattern, with exquisite cutting completely covering the surface of the glass. Such patterns appeared on complete table settings and decorative pieces for all areas of the home. By 1906, however, the rising cost of production and the waning interest of the public in ornately cut glass caused the factories to turn to simpler designs (Ill. 5).

The Brilliant and Flower periods overlap to a great extent. While one company continued the overall cutting of geometric patterns, another might move on to engraving. Still others cut transitional pieces with both geometric figures and engraving. Because of this gradual transition between the two periods, the problem of dating such transitional glass becomes complicated. Consequently these pieces must be dated by pattern and depth of cutting rather than by the period (Ill. 6).

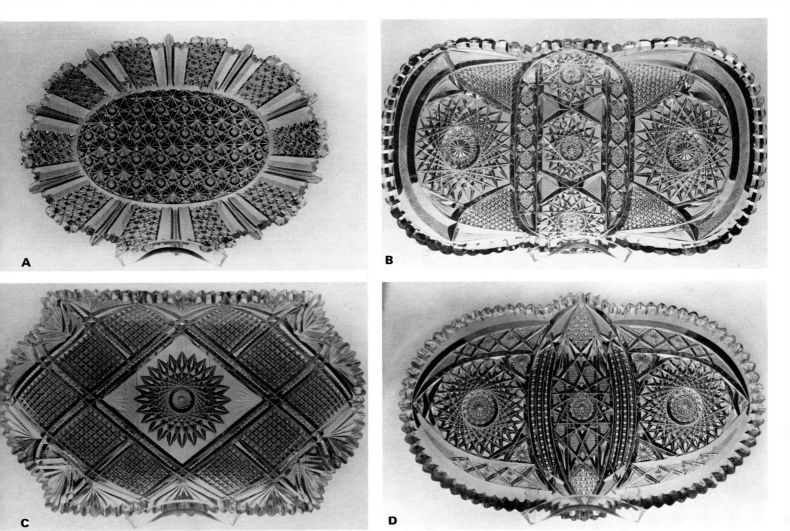

4. Four trays that demonstrate the early overall cutting of the Brilliant Period. **A.** The 10-inch oval tray by Pairpoint is in the Persian variation of Russian pattern. Hawkes patented the original Russian pattern on June 20, 1882. **B.** An ice cream tray, 15 inches long, shows the trend toward more variety in motifs, as it uses the hobstar, crosshatching, and diamonds. *George Clark.* **C.** A 14-inch ice cream tray with blocks of strawberry-diamond, an early motif. **D.** A 12-inch tray combines beading, cane, and single stars, as minor motifs, with hobstars. *Sharalyn Spiteri*

5. Pieces showing the minute cutting that developed at the height of the Brilliant Period. **A.** The 10-inch shallow bowl has a hobstar center expanding into a border of alternating hobstars and 8-point stars. *Aubright Collection.* **B.** An 8-sided platter, 15 inches, that resembles Egginton's Calvé pattern. *Aubright Collection*

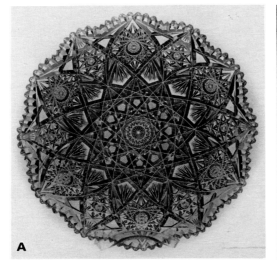

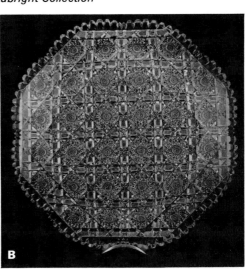

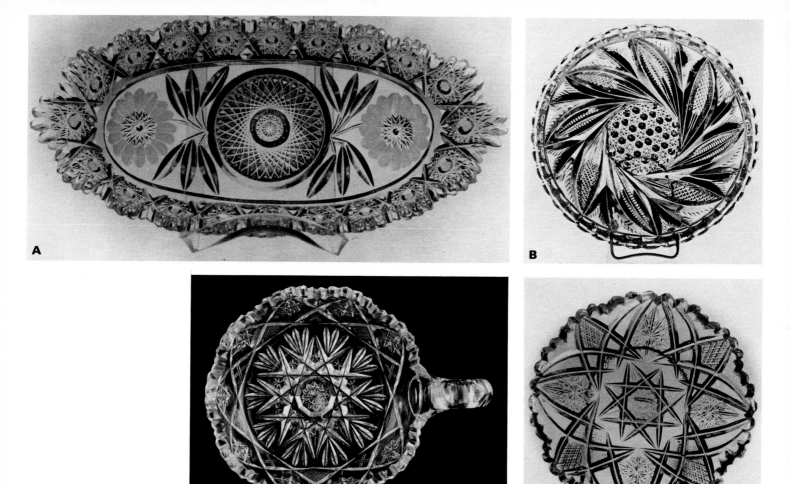

6. Four pieces showing the transition from the Brilliant to the Flower Period. **A.** Although hobstars dominate this 11-inch celery tray, the daisy makes an appearance. *Walker Collection.* **B.** A 6-inch nappy with the characteristics of both the Brilliant and Flower periods. *George Clark.* **C.** On this nappy signed Hoare, 6 inches, there is a flat star border and fans replace part of the hobstar on the base. **D.** A 9-inch plate, signed Fry in the center, displays the scanty cutting of geometric motifs that marked the transition to flowers only. *Mrs. Jack Pelzner*

The Flower Period (1906-1916) introduced copper wheel cutting of engraved glass. Although the craftsman turned to all forms of nature—birds, insects, and plants—as sources for his designs, the flowers so dominated the designs that most people refer to this era as the Flower Period (Ill. 7).

The glass factories still used lead in their glass formulas, but they began more and more to substitute a figured blank for the undecorated one. To make a figured blank, the glassblower blew the glass into a mold that contained part of the design. These blanks reduced the cost of cutting, as the craftsman cut only the flowers and not the leaves. You can easily recognize a figured blank by the slightly grayish color and the "greasy" feel of the molded parts. Not all factories used the figured blank; some glass of pure artistry was made during the engraving period, as well as glass of poor quality.

Making the Glass Blank

No one knows who first made glass, but evidence points to Syria and Mesopotamia as the places of origin, possibly about 2000 B.C. Later, Egypt became the nucleus of glass manufacture, and the Phoenician traders carried information about the process to all parts of the Mediterranean area. Although

7. These pieces from the Flower Period show the phasing out of the heavy cutting. **A.** An 8-inch Morgan pattern bowl has a daisy border and a band of Harvard on a figured blank. **B.** The 7-inch spoon tray uses only the flowers. *Roy Brown.* **C.** The 10-inch tray uses snowflakes with stars and fans; very late cut. **D.** This tray leaves much space uncut in the simple design of fans and buzz stars between curved miters. *Rita Klyce*

the glass formula of modern times still employed essentially the same ingredients as were used by the ancient people, American glassmen greatly improved the quality of the *metal* (molten glass). From the beginning, factories in the United States had access to an abundance of pure fine-grained sand or silica relatively free of iron oxide for making glass. Natural gas and, later, petroleum provided controlled temperatures that produced a better fusing of the ingredients. Finally, Americans added a new ingredient to the formula—lead.

White sand or silica is the basic ingredient of glass. The formula varies with the company and the country. A number of sources give the ingredients of American cut glass as silica, potash, lead oxide, niter, arsenic, and manganese. In American factories, the amount of lead, one of the most important ingredients, ranged from 35 to 50 percent. Most glass experts agree that H. C. Fry made the finest lead blanks, but he never divulged his formula nor revealed the amount of lead or the fusion temperature.

The quality of a glass blank depended on two factors: the removal of impurities and a correct combination of ingredients. The English used more soda in their glass; consequently, it had a slightly yellow cast and weighed less than the American product. The Irish and the Bohemians employed a combination

8   of potash and lime; their blanks showed a slightly gray tone. Potash and soda make glass more fusible, but lime gives it hardness. The Venetians favored a combination of soda and lime. The Americans combined potash and oxide of lead to produce a fusible heavy crystal with high refractory power. This product surpassed glass made by Europeans.

As a rule, all glassmakers used the same decoloring agents, manganese and arsenic, to remove any iron from the silica. A present-day factory, the Riedal Glass Company in Kupstein, Austria, gave us this formula for glass blanks when we visited there:

> 70% sand
> 15% nitrate of soda
> 15% lime

Every new batch, regardless of the amount of each ingredient, required thorough mixing with a large amount of powdered glass, or *cullet,* to assure smoothness.

It took judgment based on long experience to assure the right fusing of the ingredients, in order to produce a fine metal. First, each ingredient required accurate measuring, and then men with wooden shovels mixed the ingredients thoroughly in a bin before putting the batch into the crucibles or pots.

Most companies used monkey pots or closed cylindrical vessels for lead glass, to keep it free of carbon fumes and other oxidation gases created in the fire chamber. Once in the pots, the batch was gradually heated to a melting point of 2500 degrees Fahrenheit. With the introduction of gas and petroleum as fuel, it was possible to achieve the controlled temperature necessary to produce the perfect metal required for brilliant glass. Then the mixture had to cool slightly from 2500 degrees until it became hard enough to gather.

Next, a workman called a *gatherer* inserted the end of an iron blowpipe into the pot and collected a ball of molten glass, the *gather.* The blowpipe could vary in length from four to six feet depending on the size of the object to be formed. After the gatherer had rolled the gather on an iron table or marver and expanded it to form a hollow ball, he handed the blowpipe to the blower, who sat on a platform in a special blower's chair or bench with long wooden arms. By blowing and rolling the pipe back and forth on the arms of the chair, the blower produced the desired shape. Some pieces he blew free; others he shaped in an iron mold called a *paste mold*, covered with a paste of resinous beeswax.

As a glass object was being fashioned, a *servitor* might reheat the glass from time to time in a small open furnace called a *glory hole.* If the object required a pedestal or handle, a footmaker or the servitor made these from a different gather collected by a *bit gatherer.* When the blower finished his job, the servitor attached a flat-top iron rod called a *pontil* to the base of the vessel with a wad of molten glass, then broke off the blowpipe.

A *gaffer,* or foreman, now gave the vessel its final and most difficult tooling. Using such simple tools as wooden paddles, pincers, and shears, he shaped and trimmed the object. Frequently he also applied the handles or pedestals the servitor had made, sheared the lip, and removed any tool marks with additional heating. Factories designated this team of men who worked together as a *shop.*

Upon completion of the blown blank, the gaffer handed it to a *take-in boy,* who used asbestos-covered pincers to carry the finished product to the annealing oven or lehr. Small objects went into one size oven, large ones into another.

The annealing kiln (or lehr) gradually cooled the object, beginning at approximately 1400 degrees Fahrenheit. This ovenlike masonry structure maintained a heat level below the sagging point of the glass. When the kiln was full, a workman sealed it for a period of several days, according to the weight of the ware, since the slightest draft would crack the glass. A Hawkes advertising booklet (circa 1890) stated:

> At the end of the day, the fire of hardwood is removed from the kiln containing the pieces of glass, and the doors are closed tightly and sealed to prevent possible draught. Thus it remains for about a week, the temperature gradually lowering until the glass is cool enough to remove.

Light pieces, like a goblet or wineglass, went into a gas-heated lehr, where they cooled gradually as they moved through a tunnel on a belt, a procedure that took about twenty-four hours. From the Hawkes advertising booklet comes this description:

> . . . some sixty feet long with a fire-box extending under about the first six feet and fed with any common fuel. . . . The ware is placed on pans, one hooked to another, resting on wheels and slowly drawn by an endless chain from the heated toward the cold end of the oven.

At the opposite end, a worker removed them.

Annealing reduced the brittleness of the glass. If it cooled too quickly, it would *fly* or show tiny hairlike imperfections or wrinkles. Such imperfections, in fact, can develop years later. We have two wineglasses signed Hawkes that have these hairlike lines. Some authorities say that such glass will eventually fly or explode into many pieces, but Otis Gerould, an old-time cutter, referred to such glass as scissile. He assured us it would never explode.

Drinking glasses or bowls actually take a global shape when blown and need cracking off to form the opening. At the Riedal Glass Company we watched a worker use a diamond point to scratch the breakage line on stemware. She applied a rotating pinpoint flame to crack off the unwanted portion. Fire polishing or grinding smoothed the rough edge. The removed glass went into a waste box for pulverizing into glass cullet for a new batch.

The process of making a blank with a colored overlay required additional work. First, the clear blank had to be blown and cooled. The craftsman then spread the molten colored glass over the surface of the clear blank, keeping the liquid color at exactly the right temperature so that it would not melt the clear blank but still would be warm enough to adhere to the surface. With too hot a mixture, the color fused with the clear and ruined it for cutting. When it was too cold, it became merely a layer of colored glass on a clear surface that would shatter or break when the cutter tried to cut the design. Most authorities refer to this type of colored glass as *overlay* glass.

Finally, a worker carefully inspected each blank, clear or colored, for defects. Pieces with flaws became cullet for a new batch. The perfect glass blanks went to the storage room to await the cutting process.

2.

ARTISTRY
ON GLASS

THE SUPERIORITY OF AMERICAN CUTTING RESULTED FROM A NUMBER OF factors. Electric-powered cutting machines gave the craftsman an even control of his work. The invention of new steel cutting wheels at this time also promoted a smoother and more controlled job of cutting. Better feeding-up brushes gave a finer polish to the glass. Experienced craftsmen such as Christian Dorflinger and Thomas Gibbon Hawkes, along with many others, immigrated to this country. American enterprise took advantage of all these favorable factors and added assembly-line procedures so that an expert handled each step of the production rather than one man doing the entire cutting job.

Throughout the history of cut glass only men—never women—ran the cutting wheels. Later, Pitkin and Brooks did hire women as light and heavy engravers. The cutting followed very precise steps, according to the late William L. Wixson, an old-time cutter who apprenticed at Libbey Glass Company and later worked for Pitkin and Brooks (Ill. 8). Many cutters began as apprentices when only twelve or thirteen years old. They looked forward eagerly to the day they would become master cutters and create new motifs and patterns on glass.

All cutting started with the pattern. William Wixson told us that the master cutter ordinarily designed a pattern. Phillip McDonald designed the Russian pattern for Hawkes. J. S. O'Connor did the Parisian for Dorflinger. A number of the master cutters, such as O. F. Egginton and H. P. Sinclaire, eventually opened their own shops.

8A. The late William L. Wixson shown with some of the glass he cut after the age of eighty. *Photo by Mooradean.* **B.** An ashtray that was specially cut for the authors, containing a buzz star, the Pitkin and Brooks heart Wixson created for that company, intaglio flowers, and hobstar center.

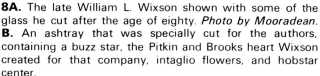

The master cutter, according to Mr. Wixson, would take a blank and begin cutting freehand (Ill. 9). Once he had completed the cutting, the company generally made a sketch or a rubbing. Sometimes a cutter would do sample pieces for others to follow. Otis Gerould said that he often created a "sample" for other cutters to use when he worked for the A. H. Heisey & Company. "When I did regular cutting, I worked from either a sample or a sketch." After he had cut the same piece several times, he no longer needed a reminder.

9A. William L. Wixson cuts a pattern he has roughed out on a bowl. *Photo by Mooradean.* **B.** This 9-inch bowl is roughed out but only partly cut and not completely polished (the unpolished area appears to be out of focus). Possibly this piece was used for a patent picture. *Hunt Collection*

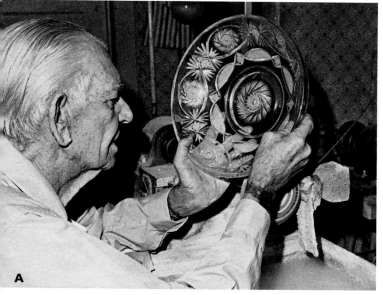

12 Workmen in the company drew the major parts of a pattern, such as the deep miter cuts, on the blanks with a gummy red or black fluid. At the Riedal Glass Company in Austria, women did this marking with red grease pencils. A Hawkes advertising catalog explained that the rougher sometimes marked the blanks before cutting was done. This rougher, probably an apprentice, cut the deep miter lines of the pattern by pushing the blank against a large, rapidly turning stone or steel wheel, watching his work through the inside of the glass. Fine wet pumice dripped from an overhanging funnel or hopper onto the steel wheel, to keep the glass surface from overheating and to help cut the blank. The stone wheel needed only water for cooling. Later, a carborundum wheel was used, as it cost less (Ill. 10).

10A. William L. Wixson cutting a goblet on a carborundum wheel. *Photos by Mooradean.* **B.** Otis G. Gerould holds a cut glass bowl he has reconditioned. Note the various sizes of cutting wheels he uses. His cutting shop occupies a double garage back of his residence.

Cutting wheels varied in thickness, diameter, and shape of the edges. A wheel with a rounded profile produced a hollow cut; a flat one did a panel, and a V-shaped one made a bevel cut. A tall board near each cutter contained all the various sizes of cutting disks and wheels. A motor with a foot control turned the wheel as the worker cut the glass.

Both roughing and smoothing required a large number of wheels. The smoother or master cutter refined the work of the rougher and created, free-hand, the intricate design on the glass. Each design required ten to twelve of his many wheels.

A stone wheel, such as a blue miter or craigeleith, was used for the fine cutting of the pattern. This wheel required frequent truing or honing with a piece of flint so that it would bring out the sharpness of the pattern. The smoother created the design by turning the glass object in various directions for deep or shallow cuts. While he cut, water dripped constantly on the wheel to prevent the glass from overheating and cracking. According to Mr. Wixson, a smoother soon learned the high-pitched sound made by the vibration of a blank just before it cracked. "A smoother needed to watch out for tiny pebbles in the pumice, too. They would cut right through the blank. . . . You get sensitive to the wheel and can feel the depth of penetration—whether a full half inch for a thick bowl or a hair's breadth in a wine glass."

The surface of the glass took on a smoky or whitish look when it was cut. **13**
This had to be polished away to reveal the brilliancy. Before 1900, the polisher
used wooden wheels of willow, cherry, or soft woods, along with a mixture of
pumice, rottenstone, and water, to produce the luster. He held the glass against
the wooden wheel while it turned through the damp pumice (Ill. 11).

For the second polishing, he used a brush wheel moistened with the same
preparation, and for the next he brushed the piece with a putty powder consisting of lead and tin. The final polishing required a cork or wooden wheel covered with a fine, moist, putty powder. Flat surfaces needed buffing with a thick
felt wheel. The lapidary cutting seen on stoppers and neck rings required three
wheels: a steel one for roughing, stone for smoothing, and lead for polishing. In
"lapping," done with the sides of various wheels, the craftsman worked freehand entirely.

With the rising cost of making cut glass at the turn of the century, every
company looked for quicker and cheaper methods of polishing glass. Mr. Wixson thoroughly disapproved of the acid bath. "It was dangerous, and it never
looked as good as hand polishing. It gave the glass a watered look on the clear
surface."

A mixture of acids was put into lead tanks, with a fan above to whip off
the fumes. First, the workman would wax the inside of the piece or any surface
not needing to be polished. Dressed in protective clothing and mask, he would
then place the pieces in a wire basket and lower it into the tank while he held a
stopwatch. Actually, the process required dipping in three different tanks, two
holding varied strengths of acid solution. The last tank contained water. In this
he dipped the item three times before setting it aside to drip dry.

The glass had to be removed from the acid bath at exactly the right time,
or the acid ate into the glass and pitted it. An acid polish, according to Mr.
Gerould, shows a graininess; it softened the sharp cuts to almost a pressed-
glass smoothness. Pieces polished by hand have a higher brilliancy and a
greater value than those done in an acid bath.

Women did the final washing, which removed all the polishing powders,
and prepared the pieces for storage. At this point an employee would acid-
stamp the signature, if any, on the article. Most likely he scratched the
numbers on the decanters and bottles fitted with stoppers. Matching numbers
were put on the stopper and somewhere on the neck of the decanter or bottle.

One skill led to the development of another. Yankee ingenuity relied on
experimentation to create new marvels in the field of glass. As one process
increased in cost, glass factories turned in new directions. Color-cut-to-clear
glass became one of the first casualties.

11. Mr. Gerould polishes a goblet he has cut. Note the water trough —it keeps the polishing wheel wet so that the glass does not overheat and crack.

14 # Colored Cut Glass

Anyone owning a piece of American colored-cut-to-clear glass has a true treasure, for prohibitive cost soon curtailed its production. A collector who has done considerable research on this glass is convinced that colored cut glass actually rated as a hobby with the company or the glass cutter. Other experts classify such glass as custom-made presentation pieces, items to be displayed at fairs and exhibitions, or special-order individual gifts. Few, if any, of these patterns appear in the available catalogs of the various companies that cut colored glass. Except for well-known patterns, such as Russian or Parisian, the designs remain unidentified. Obviously, some pieces must have appeared in the regular line even though in limited quantity.

As a rule, Americans used patterns with some uncut surface so that the color would dominate. Russian pattern, however, proved the exception; you can hardly see the color on it (Ill. 12). The favorite patterns and motifs were Strawberry-Diamond and Fan, Parisian, Harvard, simple hobstars, or thumbprints combined with hobstars. A collector we interviewed owns several pieces of cranberry overlay with an intaglio cut.

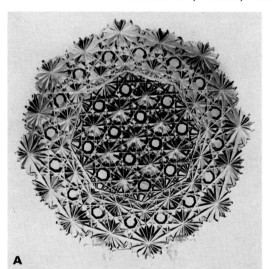

12. Three pieces of the very rare colored-cut-to-clear glass. The combination of colored and clear glass makes the curving sides of the pieces appear out of focus. **A.** An 8-inch plate in blue-cut-to-clear Russian. *Argie Burwell.* **B.** A 9-inch ruby bowl cut-to-clear by Bergen; patent date, August 3, 1896. *George Clark.* **C.** A 4 ½-inch finger bowl in cranberry-cut-to-clear. *George Clark*

Because of the cost of production, glass factories produced only certain specific colored pieces. Colored cut glass wine sets, punch sets, bowls, nappies, water carafes, vases, and plates are the most common (Ill. 13).

The lead used resulted in a vibrant color that foreign glass lacked. Most authorities agree that American factories made colored cut glass in green, ruby, amber, blue, cranberry, amethyst, and rainbow. Rainbow, the rarest of all, blended three or more colors. We have seen more of the colored-cut-to-clear in ruby, green, and blue, but another collector of colored-cut-to-clear glass owns a piece in pink and a compote in solid amber on a metal stand, heavily cut and signed "Pairpoint." Another collector owned a green decanter in the Wheeler pattern by Mt. Washington Glass Company (Ill. 98).

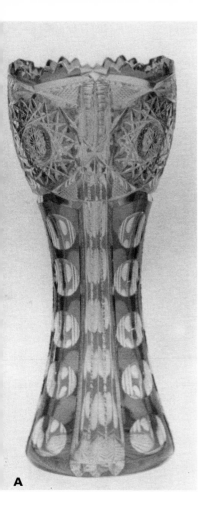

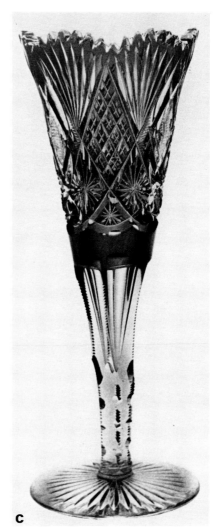

13. Vases and decanters seemed to be favorites with some companies. **A.** A 10-inch cranberry vase with hobstar border and lines of thumbprints, a favorite design in color. *George Clark.* **B.** Cranberry-cut-to-clear wine decanter. Note how the stopper repeats the design of the decanter. *Marie H. Hegarty.* **C.** Vase, 12 inches high, in Harvard by Libbey was shown in their 1893 catalog. It has a ruby overlay.

Not too many companies signed colored cut glass, as a rule. We have seen only a picture of a water carafe in cobalt blue signed "Fry," but have examined punch cups in green signed "Clark." Although some doubt exists that Libbey ever cut this type of colored glass, one collector owns wineglasses in red cut to clear and signed "Libbey" with the sword. Hawkes also signed a number of pieces.

Authorities agree that the following companies produced colored-cut-to-clear glass: C. Dorflinger & Sons, T. G. Hawkes & Company, H. C. Fry Glass Company, Pairpoint Corporation, Bergen Cut Glass Company, Libbey Glass Company, and T. B. Clark & Company. Possibly other companies cut some, but we have not been able to verify this. Most collectors and dealers endeavor to identify a piece of colored cut glass by the pattern from information in patent records, old catalogs, or magazine articles. Old catalogs do identify a number of designs created by Pairpoint and Libbey. A patent record verifies a Bergen piece.

Silver Decoration

Silver added richness and variety to cut glass. A number of companies put silver rims on bowls, pitchers, and compotes, to prevent chipping as well as to beautify them. Vases and urns often were given a silver base to add weight and so prevent spills and tipping. Silver always formed the serving parts of punch ladles and salad sets. Dresser jars and desk pieces often had silver lids, and decorative silver bands were put on hinged boxes. Some decanters have silver-decorated stoppers; Worcestershire Sauce bottles and barber bottles had silver and cork stoppers, and silver formed the top and handle of syrup pitchers and capped salt and pepper shakers (Ills. 14 and 15).

As a rule, the glass factories put sterling silver on the finer-cut pieces and plate on the less expensive ones. Pairpoint, Meriden Cut Glass Company (later International Silver Company), Hawkes, and Dorflinger, to name a few, produced their own silver parts. Others hired silver companies to make lids, stoppers, and other accessories for them. The word *sterling* indicates the silver is American. On some silver plate you will find such terms as *triple* or *quadruple*. They indicate a heavier coating of silver, but such pieces are not as highly priced as those with sterling decoration.

14. Silver fittings add a touch of elegance. **A.** A most unusual stoppered water carafe with a silver neck. *Tisnado Collection.* **B.** The silver rim on the 11-inch champagne pitcher adds to the beauty of the piece and protects the glass edge. *Hebel Collection*

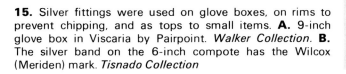

15. Silver fittings were used on glove boxes, on rims to prevent chipping, and as tops to small items. **A.** 9-inch glove box in Viscaria by Pairpoint. *Walker Collection.* **B.** The silver band on the 6-inch compote has the Wilcox (Meriden) mark. *Tisnado Collection*

Intaglio Decoration

"Intaglio" refers to any kind of recessed carving with stone or copper wheels, the opposite of cameo work. Instead of geometric designs, the engraver carves freehand figures or flowers. The copper wheels varied in size from a pinhead to six inches. Wheels as thin as a hair or a quarter-inch thick were used to cut away or carve the surface. An engraver might use fifty or more small copper wheels (Ill. 16).

The engraving wheel was attached to the end of a steel rod fastened in a lathe. As it revolved rapidly, a drop of oil or emery powder was fed onto it from time to time. In this type of decorating the artisan worked with the copper wheel between him and the glass object. With cut glass the artisan kept the blank between him and the stone wheel. If the engraver so desired, he could first outline the design with a steel pin. Engraving, like cutting, left the glass with a smoky or white appearance. Most companies did not completely buff out the white but left the engraving silvery. Hawkes completely restored the cut surface to its original clarity, and designated such pieces "rock crystal" (Ill. 17). Thinner blanks were used for engraved decoration than for regular cut glass.

The engraver used the natural stone wheel for deeper and larger carvings. Donald Parsche says, "During the cut glass period *intaglio* usually meant stone cutting, and craftsmen referred to the work as *intaglio cut* rather than engraving." A slight polishing left the design a silvery gray, in contrast to the clarity of rock crystal.

Intaglio designs depicted a cluster of fruit, flowers, butterflies, berries, or other natural objects. Frequently the artisan would combine intaglio cutting with geometric figures on such decorative pieces as powder boxes, cologne bottles, and sweetmeat jars. The high cost of intaglio work restricted its use mostly to ornamental pieces rather than tableware (Ill. 18).

Hawkes referred to his intaglio cutting as *gravic glass*, and he created pieces of rare distinction. Most of his pieces bore the acid-etched signature "Hawkes Gravic Glass."

16. Two candlesticks illustrate deep cutting and copper wheel engraving. **A.** A 9-inch candlestick in Fancy Prism by Hawkes. *Irma Adams.* **B.** A 9-inch candlestick in copper wheel engraving by Libbey.

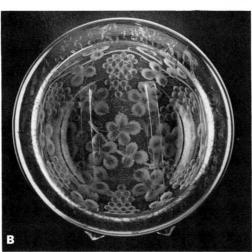

17. As buyers' interest in heavy cutting waned, Hawkes began to hire more engravers. This engraved vase measuring 8 inches in height is signed "Joe Lalonde," probably the name of the designer. "Hawkes" appears on the silver base. *Tisnado Collection.* **B.** Sinclaire bowl in Grapes pattern, 8 inches. *Tisnado Collection*

18. Intalgio always catches the eye of the collector. **A.** An 8-inch relish dish intaglio cut in Tuthill Grapes, Pears, Cherries, and Oranges. **B.** A 10-inch bowl signed "Hawkes Gravic Glass" in the Three Fruits pattern. *Helen Breeding*

3.

IDENTIFICATION
BY MOTIF

CUT GLASS, LIKE ANY ANTIQUE, SPEAKS A LANGUAGE OF ITS OWN. FOR EX-
ample, in any antiques magazine you can read advertisements for cut glass
similar to these two:

> Cut glass 12″ in diameter flower center, hobstar, rosette, strawberry diamond,
> double lozenge, St. Louis neck, large double hobstar base. Mint. Good blank.
>
> *or*
>
> Signed Clark ice bucket with two handles, double notched. Motifs of hobstars,
> crosshatching, cross-cut diamonds, 20-point hobstar on base. 5″ tall by 9″ to tip
> of handles. Excellent quality. Mint.

Unless you know the language, however, you cannot visualize these pieces.
Much of the information in such advertisements is a listing of the motifs cut on
the glass.

The word *motif* refers to a single figure cut on a piece of glass. A *design* or
pattern is a combination of several motifs. As a rule, a pattern contains one
dominant and one or more minor motifs, but a few early patterns used only one
dominant motif, such as the block or hobnail.

For years dealers and collectors described a piece of cut glass by the dominant motif, perhaps a hobstar or pinwheel. Since collectors and buyers wanted
a more accurate description, some dealers now describe both the major and the
minor motifs, as can be seen in the sample advertisements. A motif may indicate the period of cutting, the intrinsic quality of the article, and occasionally
the identification of the glass house.

The Line Motifs

The simplest motifs developed from straight-line cuts. As the artisan grew more skilled, these lines were used as the framework for the dominant motif. Around 1900 the cutter notched the ridges between parallel lines to form a dominant motif.

Blaze or Fringe

The Americans borrowed this simple line motif from the English and Irish. In it the vertical lines of shallow cuts run parallel and form a border that resembles fringe. By varying the length of the lines, the cutter could create a round or pointed scallop along one edge. The Americans cut the blaze as a minor motif to accent a dominant one.

Although the blaze seems to have been most popular in the early years of the Brilliant Period, a number of companies revived it later in a different form. Dorflinger accented flowers by cutting a blaze around the petals. Tuthill Cut Glass Company placed the blaze around the fan. Others used it to outline leaves, buzzes, and various other motifs (Ill. 19).

Step

The step motif consisted of horizontal lines in a parallel arrangement that suggested a stairway. Borrowed from the English and Irish, this motif also appeared early in the Brilliant Period. Later, cutters trimmed the necks of water carafes, the spouts of pitchers, or the pyramidal stands of compotes with these parallel lines (Ill. 20).

Miter

A miter is a deep, V-shaped incision in the glass. In most cases it outlined and unified the design. The early miters were straight lines, but with the introduction of gas and electricity to power the cutting wheel, the curved miter took over. Most authorities credit Dorflinger with introducing the curved miter in the Parisian pattern designed by John S. O'Connor and patented May 4, 1886 (Ill. 21).

The miter has appeared in many different forms during all periods of cut glass, as both a major and minor motif. Curved miters intersected to form the "vesica," a pointed oval. Sometimes a miter will split the vesica lengthwise.

19. The blaze accented other motifs. **A.** On this 7-inch plate the blaze outlines the thumbprint. *Alice Peri.* **B.** The blaze accents the fan on a 6-inch plate signed Tuthill. *Hebel Collection.* **C.** On a 10-inch shallow bowl the blaze follows the outline of the flowers. *Argie Burwell*

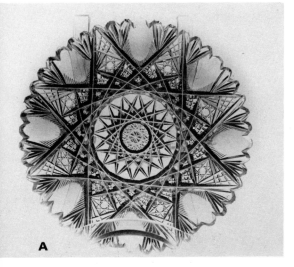

20. Three pieces showing the use of the step motif. **A.** A water carafe has steps around the neck, to produce a firmer grip. *Rita Klyce.* **B.** Steps decorate the base of the compote. *George Clark.* **C.** A pitcher 8 inches tall is deeply cut with steps at the neck. *George Clark*

21. Bowls showing the extensive use of the miter. **A.** On this 9-inch bowl the miters form panels for flat stars; the design resembles Hawkes's. **B.** Straight miters radiate from a hobstar center to a band of small hobstars similar to designs by Hoare. **C.** On this 8-inch bowl signed Hoare the curved miters form intersecting ovals. *Roy Brown.* **D.** Curved miters frame hobstars on this 10-inch bowl. *Aubright Collection*

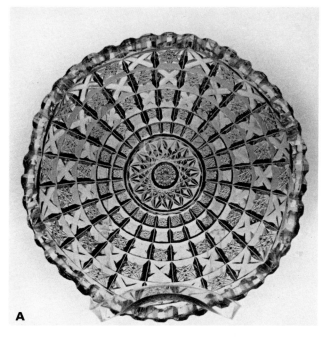

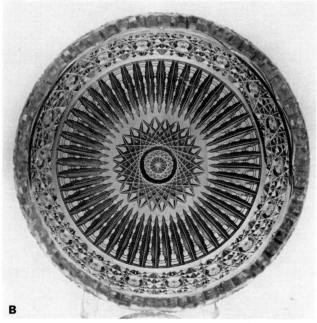

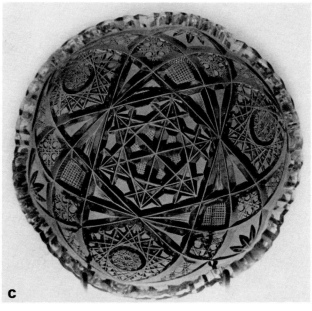

22 T. B. Clark & Company angled lines into the miter for a plume or the frond of fern. A very popular miter motif consisted of a double lozenge, an oblong diamond divided in the center with an X. The cutter usually crosshatched the space between the X and the point. Sometimes the cutter separated the diamonds of the lozenge with double X's framing a hobstar (Ill. 22).

Fan

To form this motif, short mitered lines were radiated from a focal point, to resemble an open fan. In all periods, cutters have trimmed glass with fans. The early fan motif contained three to five prongs, but the number varied from seven to nine in the Brilliant Period. At that time the fan not only still functioned as a border but was also used to fill any otherwise undecorated part of the surface, to balance the design (Ill. 23).

Designers soon discovered new ways to complicate this simple motif. For example, they placed other fans between the prongs, to make a "flashed fan." Some notched the ridges between the fan miters. Others placed two or more fans together to form a partial circle. In fact, the fan and its variations ranked as one of the more indispensable minor motifs of all periods.

Beading

This motif was made by cutting two long miters close together and notching the space between them so that it resembled a string of beads. If the miters were curved, the notches took a round or oblong shape. Several lines of beading might appear together. This motif appeared mostly in the Brilliant Period, frequently on tall pitchers (Ill. 24).

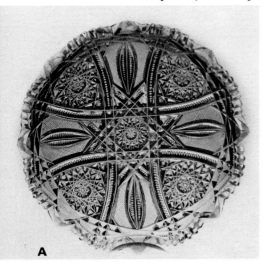

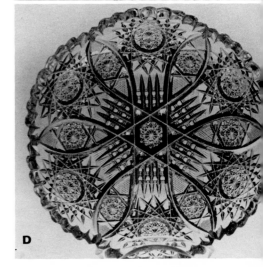

22. Vesicas and lozenges gave variety to heavily cut designs. **A.** The 10-inch bowl listed as Webster pattern in the Higgins & Seiter catalog shows a split vesica alternating with a hobstar. *Garth Mowery.* **B.** An 8-inch plate uses another version of the split vesica. It is signed Clark near the center. **C.** This 10-inch shallow bowl has lozenges formed with curved miters and crosshatching. *Thelma Prouse.* **D.** A double-X lozenge on this 9-inch shallow bowl alternates with the hobstar. *Barbara W. Doble*

A

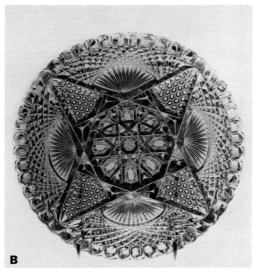

B

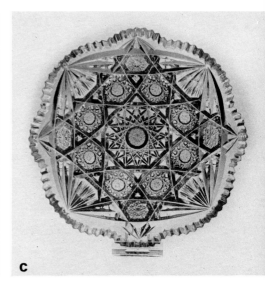

C

23. Fans offered unlimited possibilities for decoration as a minor motif. **A.** A 10-inch plate signed Hoare uses flashed fan to frame the diamonds. *Walker Collection.* **B.** Fans with 15 prongs separate the points of the star on this 7-inch plate signed Hoare. *Barbara W. Doble.* **C.** This 8-inch bowl substitutes fans for the rosettes in Festoon pattern. **D.** Elongated fans radiate from the center of a 7-inch plate.

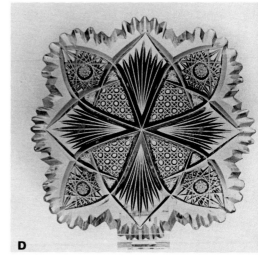

D

24. Beading and the St. Louis diamond used as accent motifs. **A.** A 12-inch vase signed Hoare has beading on four sides. *Roy Brown.* **B.** Water carafe with St. Louis diamond decoration on the neck is not only beautiful but the neck can be gripped firmly. **C.** The champagne pitcher, 11 inches in height, has beading on either side of the handle and in front.

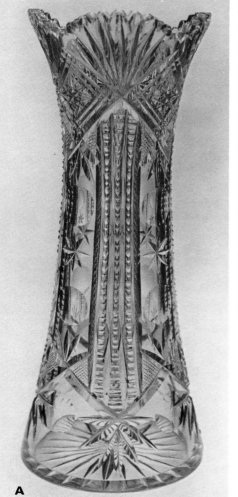

A

B

C

Geometric Motifs

European glass designers copied geometric figures but kept them simple in form. By contrast, the Americans—highly competitive—took the same geometric figures and developed them into ornate motifs.

Diamond

The diamond, very popular in all periods of cut glass, developed into a variety of forms. Perpendicular miters formed the square base and tapering sides of the minute "nailhead" or pointed diamond. This tiny pointed diamond, taken from English designs, became a minor motif early in the Brilliant Period. It functioned as a border or filled in patches of undecorated surface, to complement a pattern (Ill. 25).

The Americans developed their own version of the pointed diamond, flattening the point of the nailhead diamond and cutting a cross on it; it became known as the "strawberry diamond." Not only the nailhead English diamond but also the American version of it was always cut in a group arrangement. At the beginning of the Brilliant Period this cross-cut diamond appeared as a major motif, but in later years it became popular as a minor one. We have seen the cross-cut diamond on the handle of a water pitcher, the handle of a basket, and on the base of a compote. Some dealers call a large strawberry diamond a "pineapple diamond" (Ill. 26).

A "relief diamond" is an enlarged version of the nailhead, although some authorities classify the two as the same. Unlike the nailhead, however, the enlarged relief diamond might share importance with another dominant motif or form the link in a chain border. On small pieces such as a mustard or ointment jar, it served as the dominant motif. The Maple City Glass Company alternated a variant of this diamond (actually, a half diamond) with a button in a square to create a heavily cut pattern (Ills. 25 and 27).

The "St. Louis diamond" consisted of hollowed-out diamonds grouped in a cluster. Some authorities refer to hexagons grouped in the same manner as a St. Louis diamond. At the beginning of the Brilliant Period, cutters did complete patterns in this motif, but later they relegated it to the necks of water carafes and to vases and spittoons (Ill. 24).

Block

In imitation of the English and Irish, the American cutter formed the block motif—raised flat-top squares—with perpendicular and parallel miters. This motif rated as a dominant one early in the Brilliant Period, but its plainness did not attract the American consumer, so cutters largely discontinued it. Some designers used it occasionally as a minor motif or in a group together as a major one.

25. The nailhead diamond appeared to be more popular as a minor motif before the turn of the century. **A.** An 8-inch water pitcher with diamond vesicas around the hobstar. *Ann Dunlap.* **B.** Diamonds and crosshatching fill the lozenge on this 15-inch champagne pitcher. *George Clark.* **C.** An 8-inch cider pitcher bears the relief diamond in two versions, one with the nailhead and one with crosshatched center.

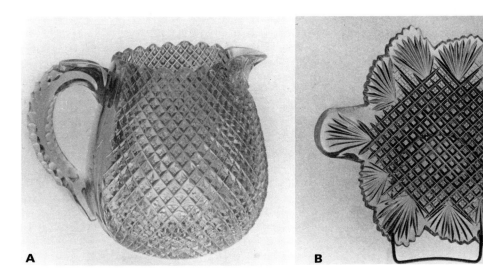

26. The strawberry diamond ranked as both a minor and a major motif. **A.** Only the strawberry diamond decorates the 5-inch pitcher (*Hebel Collection*), but the 9-inch leaf (**B**) is cut with the strawberry diamonds and fans *(Rita Klyce).*

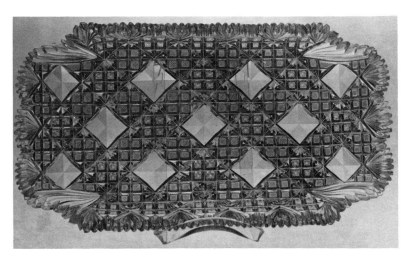

27. A 15-inch tray with relief diamonds in clear squares surrounded by small blocks of crosshatching with single stars at the points.

26 *Hobnail*

This motif consisted of a flat-top hexagon button resembling the hobnail of a heavy boot. Some cutters left the hobnail clear; others decorated it. It ranked as a major motif at the onset of the Brilliant Period but as a minor one in later years. The hobnail won great popularity as the button in the Russian, Cane, and Harvard patterns (Ill. 28).

Crosshatching

In cutting crosshatching, the cutter filled the inner area of a geometric figure with minute parallel lines that intersected at right angles. The English placed four of these crosshatched squares together and called the arrangement a strawberry diamond. Crosshatching spanned all periods of cut glass but only as a minor motif. It has become a favorite design of modern imported cut glass, often left unpolished and rather rough (Ill. 29).

28. The hobnail or button, large and small, was worked into many different designs. **A.** An 8-inch bowl uses cane in the vesicas. **B.** Similar bowl, 9 inches, increases the number of vesicas of cane. **C.** A 6-inch nappy uses patches of Harvard with hobstars. *Ardene Fairchild Smith.* **D.** On the 10-inch bowl bands of Harvard radiate from the center to the hobstars. *Thelma Prouse*

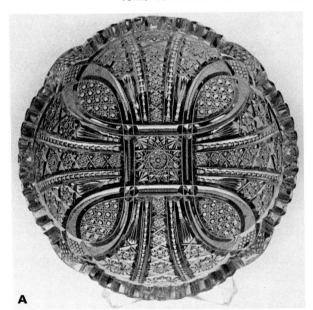

A

B

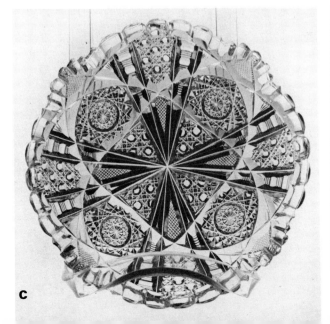
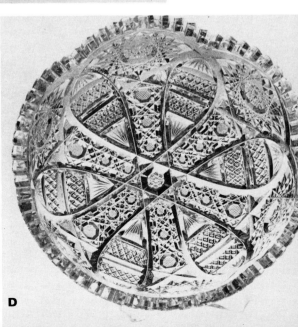

C

D

A

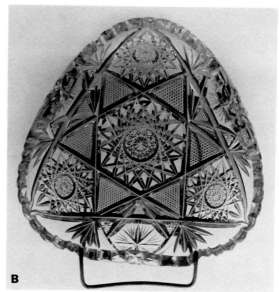

B

29. Of all the minor motifs, crosshatching seemed the most popular with the cutter. **A.** A 13-inch ice cream tray has triangles of crosshatching separating the hobstars. *Tisnado Collection*. **B.** On this triangular nappy the points of the star are crosshatched. **C.** Crosshatching is worked into the center of a 7-inch plate, to prevent bruises.

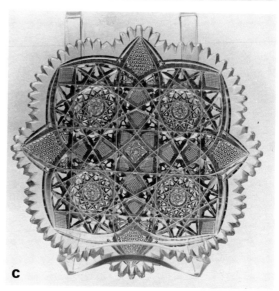

C

Key

In the transition between the Brilliant and the Flower Period, a number of glasshouses used the Greek or Roman key as a border. Meriden Cut Glass Company favored an overlapping six-sided figure as the key. Henry P. Sinclaire Company simplified the form to a chain of squares, alternately dropping the top or the bottom line of the squares (Ill. 30).

30. Meriden Cut Glass Company greatly popularized the Greek key. **A.** A 7-inch tray in Alhambra pattern has the Greek key as a border. *Sharalyn Spiteri*. **B.** An oddly shaped 11-inch bowl in the same pattern.

A

B

28   *Thumbprint*

The "thumbprint" originated with the Europeans, who called it bull's-eye or punty. It is merely a concave circle or oval. Early in the Brilliant Period, American artisans gave this motif considerable importance, but later they relegated it to handles in rows of one, two, or three (Ills. 13 and 31).

Flute

A "flute" is a vertical panel with either a flat or a concave surface. A simple pattern involving flutes was called Plain Flute by Libbey; Dorflinger referred to it as Colonial Flute. Hawkes and Clark also cut a similar design. Half flutes, borrowed from the Bohemians, proved popular as border designs on pieces cut by Tuthill and Dorflinger. Normally, flutes appear on the necks of water carafes, decanters, and cruets; on the spouts of pitchers, and on stems or pedestals. In the Brilliant Period the cutter notched the edges between the flutes. Sinclaire revived the simple flute pattern in the Flower Period, combining it with copper wheel cutting.

31. Two matching water carafes show the use of thumbprints and miters. The miniature is signed Clark on the base. *Walker Collection*

Star

Of all the geometric motifs, none formed so integral a part of all periods or offered so much variety as the star. In a number of instances, the type of star can indicate the period as well as the quality of the cutting.

The "single star" consisted of an indefinite number of single miter cuts of equal length extending from a focal center. The ends of the miters have no connection with one another, and so the name "star" applies loosely. The single star appeared in both Brilliant and Flower periods as the decoration on the base of stemware, pedestal pieces, and bowls. Master cutters devised a number of varieties. Hawkes and Dorflinger varied the length of the rays in an eight-point star on the base of a piece. Hawkes even adapted this eight-point star as a border. Clark combined the single star as a minor motif with the pinwheel.

A

B

A

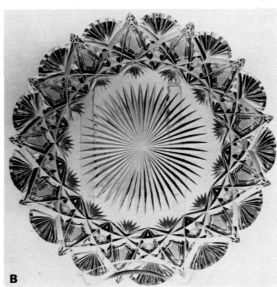

B

C

D

32. Flutes dominated the necks of decanters and vases. **A.** Notched flutes form the neck of this 11-inch wine decanter. *George Clark.* **B.** On an 11-inch vase, flutes extend from the sawtooth rim to the cutting design. *George Clark*

33. Stars came in many varieties. **A.** On this 12-inch plate, the points of the single star in the center are varied in length to give a 6-point effect. *Tisnado Collection.* **B.** The single star on this 12-inch plate is the kind that appears most often on bases. *Argie Burwell.* **C.** The shooting star on this 6-inch nappy alternates with a hobstar variation. *Ann Dunlap.* **D.** Here the shooting star forms the focal center of a nappy signed Libbey. *Rita Klyce*

30

The "shooting star" deepened the miter cuts of the single star, reduced them to approximately eight points, and inserted fans between the prongs. It appeared as a dominant motif during the transition between the Brilliant and the Flower periods. L. Straus & Sons, Libbey Glass Company, H. C. Fry Company, and J. D. Bergen Company, to name a few, cut this star as a dominant motif.

To make a "pyramidal star," the craftsman surrounded the single star with a deep miter cut so that each ray became a raised elongated triangle. Hawkes popularized this motif in the Russian pattern, but other factories devised numerous patterns using it (Ills. 12, 53).

The "flat star" developed from lines crisscrossed back and forth to create an eight-point star. In some versions the two rays at midpoint extend farther than the others. J. Hoare and Company elongated four midpoint rays. Most designers considered this a minor motif; it came in after 1900. Hoare frequently built a border of elongated stars. Other artisans placed flat stars in a type of cluster. During the Flower Period the motif increased in popularity because it reduced cutting costs. Modern imported cut glass leans heavily on this motif, leaving it intentionally unpolished for a decorative effect.

The "hobstar," so called because of its raised center, served as a dominant motif in both the Brilliant and Flower periods of cut glass, but the actual structure changed with time. Deep-cut intersecting lines formed the points of the hobstar and the facet center, the number of points corresponding to the number of facets. The points varied in number: eight, ten, twelve, sixteen, twenty, twenty-four, and thirty-two, depending on the size and shape of the piece and the period of cutting. A pyramidal star within a hobstar decorated the raised center (Ill. 35).

Dorflinger, Hawkes, Hoare, and Clark early popularized the eight-point hobstar. The top of the facet center varied with the cutter: clear, crosshatched, single star, flat, or hobstar (Ill. 36).

34. The flat star cost less to cut. **A.** Flat stars decorate this 10-inch-high rose bowl on a pedestal. **B.** An 11-inch champagne pitcher, signed Libbey on the flat of the handle, uses a flat star between two hobstars with raised centers.

A   B

A

B

35. Two ice cream trays show different uses of the hobstar in a design. **A.** A 17-inch ice cream tray with two large hobstars. *George Clark*. **B.** Three different sizes of hobstars appear on this ice cream platter, which measures 15 inches. *George Clark*

36. Cut glass dinner bells were quite popular. **A.** An 8-point star appears on this 6-inch dinner bell. *George Clark*. **B.** A 5½-inch bell with elongated star and fluted handle; this was cut much later than the other one. *Rita Klyce*

A

B

As the Brilliant Period moved toward total cutting of the glass surface, the points of the hobstar increased to twenty-four or the ultimate of thirty-two with the characteristic facet center. Some craftsmen cut the hobstar so heavily that it has a stereoscopic appearance. Hoare and O. F. Egginton arranged tiny hobstars in clusters. Others made a border of hobstars.

With the increased costs of production toward the end of the Brilliant Period, there were fewer points in the hobstar and the center was so shallowly cut that it looked more like a flat single star. Libbey combined this late hobstar with the old one in a number of patterns.

The most ornate of the hobstars became known as the "rosette." The deep and intricate cutting so raised the hob center that it resembled an actual rosette. Mt. Washington Glass Company, Hawkes, Egginton, and Sinclaire created patterns in this motif at the height of the Brilliant Period (Ill. 37).

The "flashed star" contained eight, ten, or twelve points, with fans placed between the points. Sometimes the pattern crosshatched the points; other times it left them clear. Always a dominant motif, the flashed star frequently appeared on the top of jewel and powder boxes with hinged lids. The center varied with the individual company, as it did in the hobstar. Libbey introduced the flashed star in the Florence pattern before the turn of the century, and it continued in popularity throughout the Brilliant Period. During the Flower Period, Meriden flattened the cutting of the flashed star (Ill. 38).

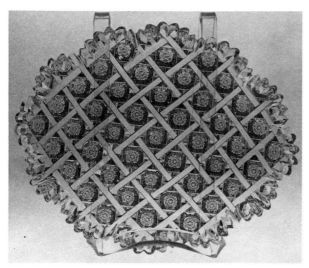

37. An 8½-inch tray showing the use of rosettes; it resembles Egginton's Calvé and Hawkes's Imperial patterns. *George Clark*

38. The flashed star was popularized by the Meriden Cut Glass Company. **A.** A 9-inch celery vase on a pedestal with the flashed star. *George Clark.* **B.** The flashed star dominates the top of an 11-inch vase. *Mrs. Jack Pelzner*

A

B

Buzz

The buzz motif appeared at the turn of the century and continued in some form until World War I. It probably received its name from its strong resemblance to a buzz saw. Like the hobstar, it was varied in numerous ways in the effort to economize on production costs.

The "pinwheel" is the more ornately cut buzz formed by curved miters and alternating fans. The heavy cutting created the illusion of a spinning wheel. This motif used the same facet center as the hobstar. Its quality depended on the number of miters and fans.

Patrick H. Healy secured a patent on a pinwheel for the American Cut Glass Company on February 28, 1899. Most authorities, however, credit Clark with its origin, since he developed it to such exceptional beauty.

In the "buzz star" the craftsman lessened the number of miters and fans and flattened the center, to decrease the cost of cutting. On occasion, Tuthill combined this motif with his intaglio patterns. Its usage marks the transition between the Brilliant and the Flower Period.

During the Flower Period the buzz or "buzz saw" further reduced the number of miters and fans, at times using no fans at all. A number of other variations appeared in the buzz motif. The American Cut Glass Company cut a fern between the curved miters. Another company put a fringe or blaze on the buzz. J. D. Bergen Company reduced the buzz points to four and added fans to the tips.

39. Four pieces showing various types of buzzes. **A.** This 10-inch shallow bowl in pinwheel is signed Clark. **B.** The large buzz star forms most of the design on an 8-inch pitcher. **C.** Four buzz stars surround the small hobstar center of this square nappy. *Tisnado Collection.* **D.** The buzz alternates with the hobstar on this 8-inch plate. *Tisnado Collection*

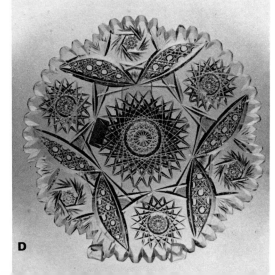

The collector should keep in mind that no sharp break occurred in the use of any motif from one period to the next; the transition was gradual. The use of these motifs depended entirely on the individual company, and the information given here is only a general guideline to their use. Perhaps no other motif than the star can so accurately date a piece as to period of cutting and its quality. In fact, the star motifs almost trace the rise and demise of brilliant cut glass.

Motifs from Nature

When interest in ornate designs began to wane and production costs rose sharply, a number of companies turned to copper wheel and stone engraving. The designer took his inspiration from nature, particularly from flowers—they characterize the years just before World War 1.

Engraved Motifs

Long before the turn of the century, Sinclaire had urged Hawkes to include copper wheel engraving in the general line. As a naturalist, Sinclaire generally sketched designs directly from nature and then transferred them to glass. Hawkes did include some of Sinclaire's creations in the exhibit at the Paris Exposition in 1889. Eventually, Sinclaire established his own company and specialized in engraved glass. Others, such as Dorflinger, Libbey, Hawkes, Pairpoint, joined the trend of glorifying nature.

Flowers ranked first in popularity, the daisy being the favorite (Ill. 40). Specific glass companies favored particular flowers. Sinclaire engraved the laurel, a symbol of peerless quality, and even used it in his signature. His engravings included the holly, rose, lily, dahlia, tulip, aster, and cornflower. The Rosaceae pattern with cut rosette band illustrates one of Tuthill's finest copper wheel engravings. Hawkes engraved the Satin Iris and Satin Carnation. Fry found the lily appealing, and others concentrated on carnations or peonies.

The copper wheel enabled the engraver to do more detailed designs in smaller areas. The more enterprising companies did not stop with flowers but included scenes, human figures, portraits, animals, birds, fish. Hawkes's scenes included the Old Oaken Bucket, a lighthouse, airplane, and ducks. Sinclaire, Hawkes, and Tuthill glorified the fish. Tuthill and other companies combined copper wheel and stone engraving (Ill. 40).

Stone Engraving

As previously explained, the stone wheel was used to cut the deep intaglio motifs so popular around the turn of the century and carried over in a limited way to the Flower Period. Tuthill used the word "intaglio" in his designs—Intaglio Poppy, Primrose, Phlox, Strawberry, or Blackberry. They commanded carriage-trade prices. Intaglio could promote a piece from the ordinary to the rare. Consequently every collector wants to include a piece of intaglio glass in his collection.

Tuthill, Sinclaire, and Hawkes probably produced the greatest amount of intaglio glass. Tuthill favored clusters of fruits or grapes as well as the flowers and butterflies. As already stated, Hawkes called his intaglio "gravic glass"; on it he used both fruit and floral patterns. Rarities include Libbey's lovebirds in the Wisteria pattern, Hawkes's ear of corn, and Tuthill's fruit cluster. Several patterns combined intaglio with heavily cut motifs (Ill. 41).

With this limited number of motifs, a master worker could create unlimited patterns of decorated glass. Many of these can be identified by name in reprints of old catalogs or by patent number.

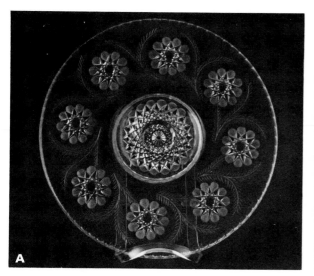

40. Some companies combined deep steel wheel cutting with engraving. **A.** A 12-inch plate in which engraved wreaths circle the flower stars. **B.** Engraved 12-inch sprigs are added to the leaves on this figured blank plate. **C.** Sinclaire's 12-inch plate in pattern #1023 uses a floral wreath around the edge to frame the deeply cut hobstars. All in *Tisnado Collection*

41. Tuthill became famous for his intaglio designs. **A.** This 12-inch plate, signed Tuthill in the center, bears a fruit design. *Tisnado Collection.* **B.** A 15-inch tray (it weighs 15 pounds and carries the Tuthill signature in the center) combines intaglio grapes with a rosette border. *Bustamente*

4.

IDENTIFICATION
BY PATTERN

IDENTIFYING CUT GLASS BY SPECIFIC PATTERN NOT ONLY OFFERS A CHALlenge but can prove to be one of the most fascinating aspects of buying and collecting. In searching through books, magazines, old catalogs, and even patent records for pattern names, however, the collector can run into considerable confusion caused by the factories themselves. Patterns were cut in numerous variations, one company altering a popular pattern only enough to avoid infringing the patent of another firm (Ill. 42).

Whenever a particular pattern appealed widely to consumers, competitors would cut a similar one. For example, Corinthian pattern proved so very popular that Straus, Libbey, Irving, and Clark each changed only one motif but kept the same general design. Straus and Libbey continued to call the pattern Corinthian. Other imitators developed their own variations, and gave them different names.

The shape of some blanks has become so closely identified with a specific company that a collector is inclined to assume only that particular factory cut those blanks. Unfortunately, many companies such as Fry, Libbey, and Dorflinger (to name a few) sold their blanks to smaller factories (Ill. 43).

In adapting a pattern to pieces of different shape, the artisan took the liberty of adding to or subtracting from the basic design. The pattern on a bowl may look different from the same pattern on a pitcher—that is, there may be one less hobstar or an additional patch of crosshatching. An artistic craftsman cared more about beauty and cutting the total surface than adhering strictly to a basic sketch, so he often cut according to the shape of a piece rather than slavishly following a design. Companies also frequently changed or simplified patterns but kept the same name (Ills. 44 and 45).

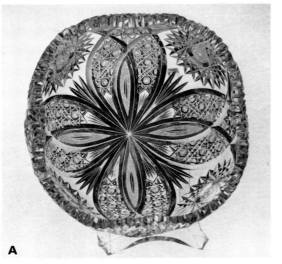

42. Two 9-inch square bowls very similar in design. **A.** Hawkes's Chrysanthemum pattern. *Rita Klyce.* **B.** A two-handled bowl that greatly resembles Lackawanna's Rosebud and Clark's Desdemona, as well as Chrysanthemum pattern. *Walker Collection*

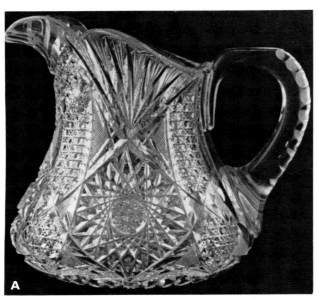

43A&B. Two pitchers cut from duplicate blanks; neither is signed. Pitchers in this shape appear in an old Libbey catalog. Both handles are triple notched.

44. From a Libbey catalog come these two versions of the Empress pattern. **A.** An 8-inch bowl in a later Libbey Empress. *Marie Hegarty.* **B.** A 7-inch relish dish in the earlier pattern, with strawberry diamond bands and hobstars rather than crosshatching and flat-centered hobstars. **C.** A heart-shaped nappy in Empress that shows a variation in shape. *Rita Klyce.* All three pieces are signed.

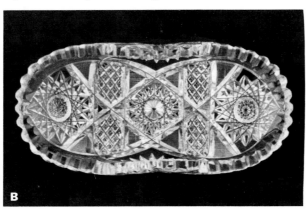

45. The two shallow 8-inch bowls (**A** & **B**) show how Hoare simplified the Hindoo pattern by substituting elongated stars for hobstars and by reducing the size of the hobstar center. Both are signed. *Roy Brown.* The design in the nappy in **C**, signed Hawkes at the dot, was greatly simplified to make the design on the one in **D**, also signed but on the inside wall. *Doris Patterson*

A number of factories advertised that they could replace broken or lost pieces. Mr. Wixson related that a woman in England mailed a piece of a punch bowl to Pitkin and Brooks and asked them to make a duplicate bowl. "I didn't know the pattern, but I followed the design as best I could. We never heard any more from her, so I guess it pleased her," he ended with a chuckle. Occasionally, the top of a lamp differs slightly from the base, or a punch bowl may not exactly match its base. In such instances, possibly someone had endeavored to replace a broken part. In any case, when one company cut a replacement for the product of another, the pattern varied.

Libbey worked as an agent for various companies, one after the other. In one sense of the word, an agent was a sales representative. A company might advertise that it served as agent for various glass companies, meaning that it handled the products of only those companies. Sometimes an agent or wholesale house used a different pattern name in their catalog from the one given by the factory. The Higgins & Seiter catalog showed a sketch of a piece identified

46. Two patterns found in catalogs of agents or wholesalers. **A.** This 6-inch berry dish signed Bergen is listed in R. T. & Company Jewelers catalog as Rye pattern. *Roy Brown.* **B.** The double-handled nappy, 6 inches wide, was listed in a Marshall Field catalog only by the number 72016.

as "Napolean" pattern that duplicated J. Hoare's Monarch. In a group of eight catalogs belonging to agents and wholesalers, we found only two that consistently used the factory pattern name. Unfortunately, this practice makes these catalogs only a secondary source of identification (Ill. 46).

According to Mr. Wixson, a glasshouse usually cut a number of sample patterns for a catalog. As the orders came in, the company produced only the patterns ordered. Consequently, some of the patterns listed by name in the catalogs never went into production.

In spite of all these problems, however, the collector should persist in his efforts to identify the patterns in his collection. There are many that can be positively identified. First, let's examine those that are in public domain.

Public Domain Patterns

A number of patterns never belonged to any particular company but from the beginning were in public domain. Other patterns started originally with a patent, but when the patent expired, the design went into public domain for anyone to cut. Most of these patterns covered the entire surface. Without a signature on pieces with public domain patterns, no one can positively identify the factory.

Notched Prism

The notching varied with different cutters. For example, Bergen used several short notches and then a long one to give a band effect. Some notched every miter, alternate miters, or every other pair of miters. A number of companies combined the notched prism with the thumbprint or the hobstar (Ill. 47).

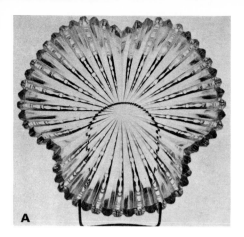

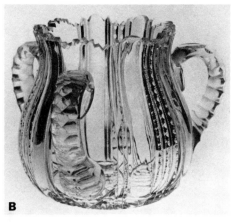

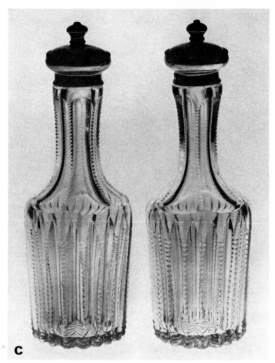

47. The simplicity of the notched prism challenged the cutter to individualize it. **A.** This 8-inch clover-shaped bowl has notching varied with a long and a short, typical of Bergen. **B.** A triple-handled loving cup, 6½ inches tall, with flutes between the prism lines. *Rita Klyce.* **C.** Simple notching appears on these bitters bottles, 5½ inches tall, with sterling silver tops. *Rita Klyce.* **D.** A 9-inch bowl groups four plain prisms between two notched ones. *Roy Brown*

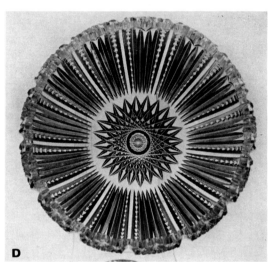

48. An 8½-inch liqueur bottle with two matching glasses, 3½ inches tall, in cranberry-cut-to-clear in a panel or flute pattern similar to Dorflinger's Panel and Heavy Flute. Note the hexagonal bases. *George Clark*

Flute

This pattern consisted entirely of concave flutes. Dorflinger and Hawkes did early patterns of this kind. Sinclaire revived the pattern and individualized it with engraving. Clark cut it with a green overlay (Ill. 48).

Honeycomb

A number of companies cut this pattern in the early years of cut glass, including Dorflinger and Hawkes.

49. Pieces showing the overall cutting of one pattern. **A.** An 8-inch-high whiskey jug in Strawberry-Diamond and Fan with matching "corncob" stopper and hobstar button on the handle. *George Clark.* **B.** An 8-inch pitcher shows the overall cutting of the hobnail. *Fannell Collection.* **C.** A 10-inch water pitcher in Harvard.

Block

Pairpoint and Smith Brothers favored this pattern.

Hobnail

Pairpoint cut this pattern extensively. Its simplicity and static nature failed to attract the American buyer (Ill. 49).

Strawberry-Diamond and Fan

This pattern covered the piece with a crosscut diamond; later, craftsmen added a fan border. According to Mr. Wixson, most companies trained apprentice cutters on this design, and so an abundance of it exists, but in varied quality. Hawkes cut the pattern extensively and signed many pieces (Ills. 49 and 50).

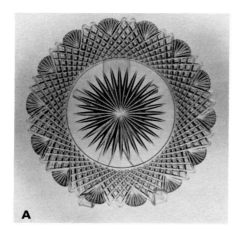

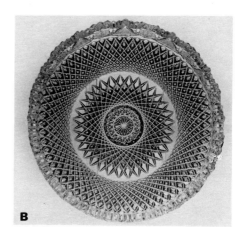

50. These two pieces show the variation in bands used with a single design. **A.** An 8-inch plate has strawberry diamonds around the rim, a single star in the center, and a fan border. *Tisnado Collection.* **B.** This 10-inch bowl makes the design more complicated, with a large hobstar center and a border of alternating hobstars and crosshatching. *Mrs. Jack Pelzner*

A **B**

51. After the turn of the century, cane became more popular as a minor motif. **A.** An 8-inch spoon tray decorated with both the cane motif and Harvard pattern. **B.** Bands of cane separate the flashed hobstars on this 10-inch bowl signed Hoare. *Jean Rieth*

Cane

Cane appeared more commonly on small or novelty items. It soon found its place in the Brilliant Period as a minor motif. Some quality pieces, such as pitchers or jugs, have Cane pattern on the handles. (Ill. 51)

Harvard

On some pieces in Harvard pattern the arrangement of the button is varied. One firm put buttons with pyramidal stars in one row and crosshatched buttons in another. Others alternated the buttons in a single row. Toward the end of the Brilliant Period and in the Flower Period, this pattern became a minor motif or shared equally with the dominant one. (Ills. 49 and 52)

Russian

Russian is the most intricately cut and possibly the best known of all patterns. Phillip McDonald, who designed it, assigned the patent to Hawkes on June 20, 1882. The Russian Embassy in Washington chose this pattern for a banquet service. In June of 1885, the American Embassy in St. Petersburg also ordered a banquet service. From these purchases came the name.

Grover Cleveland at the White House chose this design in 1886 for use at state dinners but requested the addition of an engraved crest with an eagle. From time to time the White House replaced and added pieces. Benjamin Harrison and William McKinley enlarged the set. Theodore Roosevelt ordered highball or iced tea glasses from Dorflinger. The pattern continued in use in the White House until 1938, when Franklin Roosevelt changed to a less expensive one.

Originally, Hawkes cut the pattern in the pyramidal star and the hobnail, covering the entire surface of a piece. Variations of the pattern developed, and even though these were given different names, most people commonly refer to all types simply as Russian. Ambassador pattern crosshatched the hobnail. Canterbury pattern placed a pyramidal star on the hobnail, but Cleveland left the hobnail clear. Persian pattern covered the hobnail with a hobstar; Polar

52. Two pieces show the heavy cutting of the Harvard pattern. **A.** An 8-inch-high compote. *Aubright Collection.* **B.** A 6-inch nappy in the same pattern. *George Clark*

Star used a large pyramidal star and a very small hobnail. Although many companies produced Russian pattern, we have seen only one piece signed, and that by Hawkes.

Some companies made even further changes in the original design. Dorflinger reduced the amount of cutting on Russian by using a 24-point star on the base of pieces. New England Glass Company (later Libbey) placed a corner fan on a square-shaped item. Pairpoint divided the pattern with clear vertical flutes. Hawkes himself varied it with ribs or pillars.

53. Here are five different variations of the Russian pattern: **A.** A 4½-inch plate in Russian Canterbury, which uses the single star on the button. *Tisnado Collection.* **B.** A 7½-inch plate in Russian Cleveland with the clear button. *Patrick Curry.* **C.** A 5-inch nappy in Hunt's Royal pattern uses the Russian Persian by placing hobstar on the button. **D.** A 7-inch plate has a large star and small button indicating the Polar Star Russian. *Tisnado Collection.* **E.** An 8-inch bowl crosshatches the button for the Russian Ambassador. *Tisnado Collection*

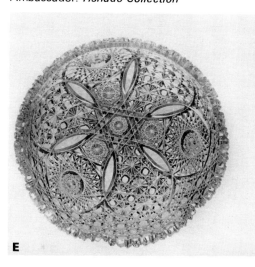

Descriptive Name Patterns

Because so many patterns have no known name, various authorities have suggested descriptive ones to aid in identifying them. Recent research and old catalogs have supplied the factory names for some of these. With others, because the names so aptly describe the pattern, dealers and collectors have continued to use them. Some such given names never became popular.

Expanding Star

No one has discovered the factory name of this pattern, but the descriptive one has become firmly established. We have seen some excellent pieces in this pattern cut on top-quality blanks, and also some very inferior cutting on poor-quality blanks (Ill. 54).

Sunburst

Many companies, among them Libbey and Bergen, cut sunburst patterns. The centers of the motif vary from crosshatching to clear thumbprint (Ill. 55).

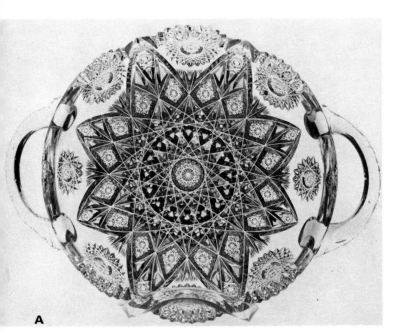

54. Expanding Star pattern does not appear in any catalogs or patent records. **A.** Double-handled tray, 12 inches. *George Clark*. **B.** Small punch bowl in Expanding Star pattern with its sterling band of grape clusters.

55. Two pieces with different types of sunburst patterns. **A.** A 12-inch flower center with the sunburst motif alternating with the hobstar. *Rita Klyce*. **B.** The sunburst on this 7-inch relish dish resembles those cut by Bergen.

Patterns and Companies

In our search to uncover the factory name for various patterns, we studied old catalogs that have become available only within recent years. While checking patent records, we discovered that the applicant himself sometimes named a design. Authoritative books on cut glass have included many of the company pattern names, and recent magazine articles have added other identifications. Unpublished catalogs from several museums have been helpful; advertisements in old magazines have supplied some names too. With the information gleaned from all these sources combined, it has been possible to pair the names of various company patterns available today with the photographs of pieces in private collections.

C.G. Alford & Company,
New York City, 1872-1918

This company operated a jewelry and watch repair store as well as a cutting shop. Some pieces have signatures, but no pattern names are available (Ill. 56).

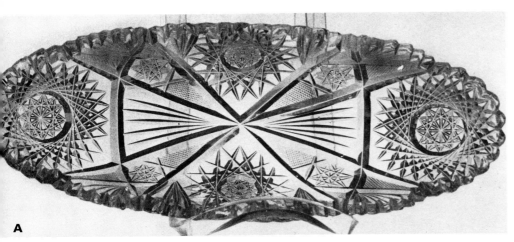

56A&B. Two very rare signed pieces by Alford: an 11-inch celery tray with hobstars and a 7 ½ -inch plate. *Walker Collection*

Almy & Thomas,
Corning, New York, 1903-ca. 1918

Charles H. Almy and G. Edwin Thomas purchased the Knickerbocker Cut Glass Company. The Corning Glass Works supplied the Almy & Thomas firm with blanks. Some collectors have signed pieces, but there is no record of pattern names (Ill. 89).

46

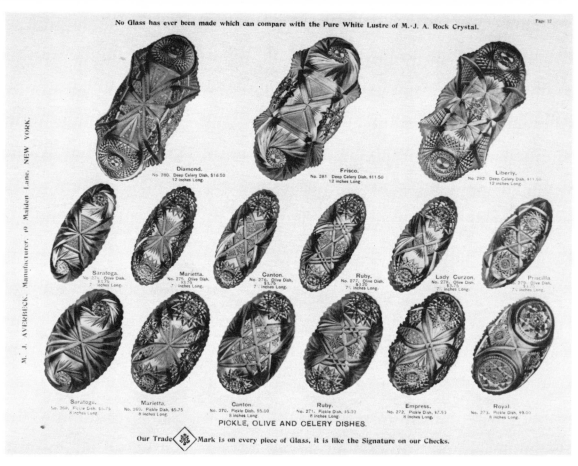

57. A page from M. J. Averbeck catalog #104, published between 1900 and 1910. *Kitty and Russell Umbraco*

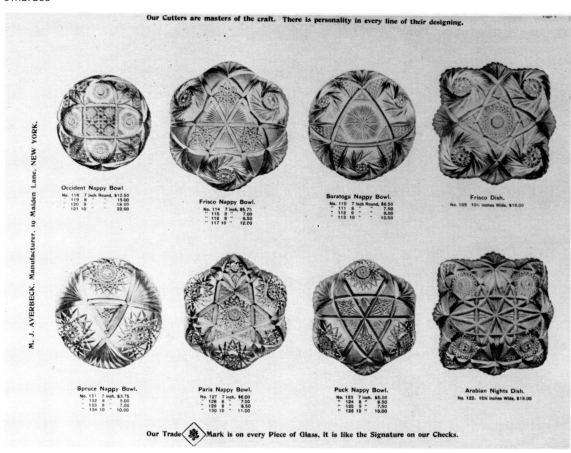

58. Another page from M. J. Averbeck catalog #104. *Kitty and Russell Umbraco*

A

B

C

59. Three patterns identified in the Averbeck catalog. **A.** 8-inch shallow bowl in Boston. *Mildred Quinn.* **B.** 4-inch miniature spoonholder in Prism. *Rita Klyce.* **C.** 6-inch plate in Spruce pattern.

Averbeck Cut Glass Company,

New York City, 1892-1923

The Averbeck family maintained a retail jewelry store and did a large mail-order business in cut glass. Their catalog guaranteed each item as "genuine cut glass" that represented "the labor of skilled artisians" by means of a trademark appearing on each piece of glass. We have seen only one signed piece. A number of such stores bought from small and relatively unknown cutting shops. Pictured are items in these patterns identified by catalogs (Ills. 57-60, 64, 89):

Azalia	Liberty
Boston	Prism
Geona	Spruce

60. The patterns of the two whiskey jugs also appear in the Averbeck catalog. **A.** Liberty is the pattern of this 6-inch jug. *George Clark.* **B.** Jug in Genoa pattern. *Walker Collection.* **C.** A 10-inch decanter in Electric pattern by Bergen, as shown in **1904-05** catalog. *George Clark*

A

B

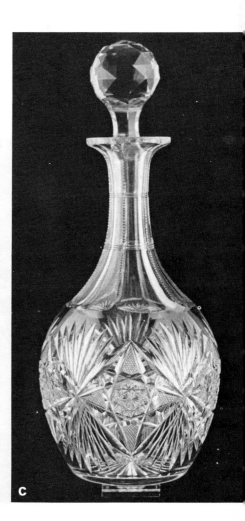

C

48 *J. D. Bergen Company,*
Meriden, Connecticut, 1880-1916

James D. Bergen worked for Mt. Washington Glass Company, New England Glass Company, and Meriden Flint Glass Company before organizing his own, along with Thomas A. Niland. In 1885, Bergen bought out Niland. Collectors and dealers have found these patterns (Ills. 61-65):

Bedford	Glenwood
Claremont	Logan
Dallas	Notched Prism
Elaine	Wabash
Electric	

61. Page from a Bergen catalog, 1904-1905. *Kitty and Russell Umbraco*

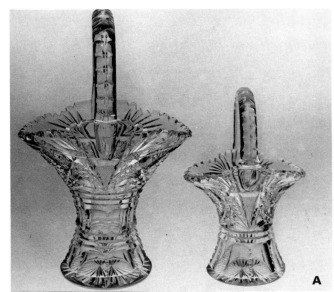

A

B

C

63. Four patterns found in the 1904-1905 and 1906 Bergen catalogs. **A.** Two baskets in Elaine, very simply cut. *George Clark.* **B.** A covered cheese dish, 9 inches high, in Glenwood. *Hebel Collection.* **C.** A large punch bowl in Wabash pattern. *Argie Burwell.* **D.** A 10-inch pitcher in Dallas.

62. Page from a Bergen catalog, 1904-1905. *Kitty and Russell Umbraco*

D

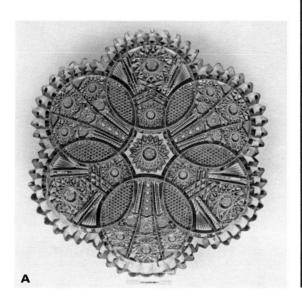

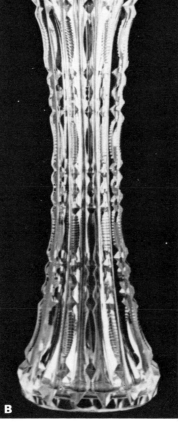

64. Three pieces identified by the 1904-1905 and 1906 Bergen catalogs: **A.** This 8-inch bowl appeared in the Averbeck catalog under the name of Azalia, in the Bergen catalog under Claremont, and in *The Pairpoint Story* as cut and signed by Lot Murray. **B.** A 6-inch vase in Notched Prism. **C.** A double-handled celery holder in Logan. *George Clark*

65. One of the most plentiful of Bergen patterns is Bedford; it is found in a number of collections. **A.** Captain's wine decanter. *Rita Klyce.* **B.** An 8-inch bowl with fluted edge.

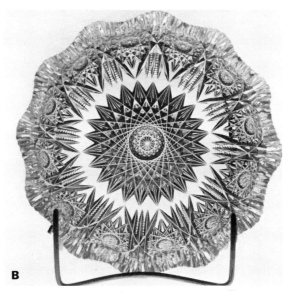

Blackmer Cut Glass Company,
New Bedford, Massachusetts, 1894-?

Arthur L. Blackmer headed this company after he worked in the business office of the Mt. Washington Glass Company. Later he worked as a salesman for the Hunt Glass Company. We have pieces in Sultana and Colombia patterns (Ills. 66 and 153).

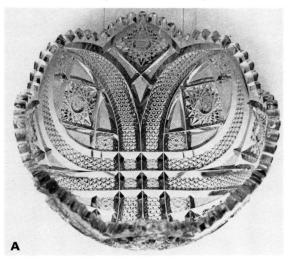
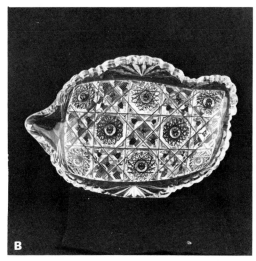

66A. The 9-inch berry bowl has intersecting cane bands in the center of the base rather than a hobstar, as shown in the original design of Blackmer's Colombia. *Thelma Prouse.*
B. Sultana is the pattern of this 7-inch relish dish by Blackmer.

T. B. Clark and Company,
Honesdale, Pennsylvania, 1884-1930

Thomas Byron Clark first worked for the Meriden Flint Glass Company before establishing a factory himself. His office headquarters was in Honesdale. Christian Dorflinger supplied the firm with blanks. In private collections we found examples of the following patterns (Ills. 67-69):

"Corinthian"	Pinwheel
Desdemona	Prima Donna
Gothic	Strawberry-Diamond and Star

The descriptive name of Prima Donna is "Triple Square."

67. Three pieces in a descriptively named pattern: Corinthian. **A.** An 8-inch shallow bowl signed Clark uses the Russian variant where Straus cut cane motif and Libbey cut the strawberry diamond. *George Clark.* **B.** This 6-inch plate signed Irving utilizes a variant of the Harvard pattern for the motif. **C.** An 8-inch compote in the same Irving pattern. *Don Carr*

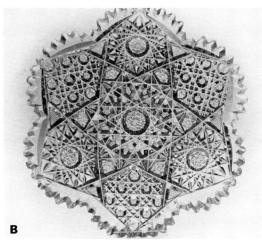

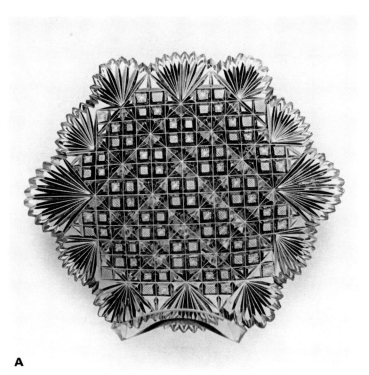

A

B

68. Three patterns signed Clark. **A.** A 12-inch shallow bowl in Strawberry-Diamond and Star, designed by Walter A. Wood and patented June 1, 1886. *Jean Rieth.* **B.** An 8-inch bowl signed Clark in Prima Donna, patented August 10, 1909. The name was located in an advertisement. *Ardene Fairchild Smith.* **C.** The dot on this 12-inch plate in Pinwheel pattern indicates the Clark signature. **D.** Another signed plate, 7 inches, is in Prima Donna pattern.

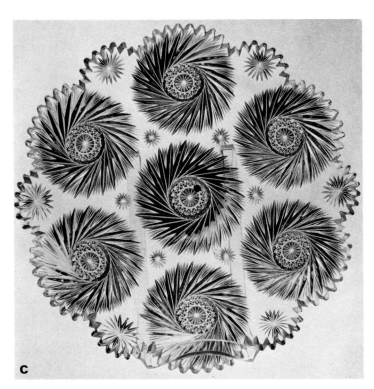

C

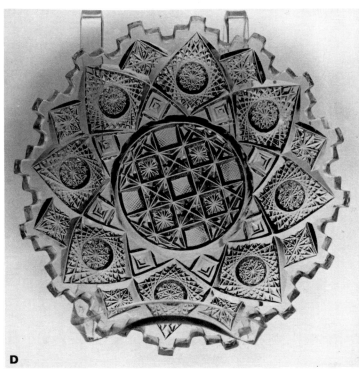

D

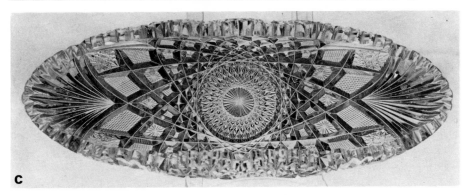

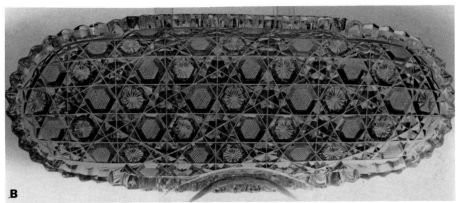

69. Three celery trays by three different glass firms. **A.** An 11-inch celery in Dorflinger's Middlesex. **B.** A Clark celery, 12 inches, in Baker's Gothic, patented September 25, 1888, by Thomas A. Baker and assigned to Clark. *Rita Klyce.* **C.** An 11-inch celery tray in Devonshire by Hawkes, patented May 8, 1888. *Mrs. Jack Pelzner*

C. Dorflinger & Sons,

White Mills, Pennsylvania, 1852-1921

Christian Dorflinger, born in Alsace, France, learned to cut in his uncle's factory at the age of ten. When eighteen he came to the United States and established a glassworks in Brooklyn that expanded into the Long Island Flint Glass Works. He retired at thirty-three because of ill health, only to open a new company in White Mills in 1865. At one time Dorflinger supplied clear and colored blanks to twenty-two cutting shops. Collectors own examples of these patterns (Ills. 69-71):

Diamond-Strawberry	Paola
Inverness	Parisian
Middlesex	No. 80

70. Four of Dorflinger's patterns: **A.** A 6 ½-inch square bowl in Diamond-Strawberry. *Sharalyn Spiteri.* **B.** A cream pitcher 4 ½ inches high in Parisian, patented May 4, 1886. *Rita Klyce.* **C.** Cereal pitcher, 5 inches tall, in #80. *C. W. Moody.* **D.** A 9-inch bowl in Paola. *C. W. Moody*

71A. The 12-inch whiskey decanter in Dorflinger's Parisian has a sterling silver stopper with Shreve (of San Francisco) on it. **B.** The vase, 15 inches in height, is Inverness pattern, shown in an undated Dorflinger catalog. *Patrick Curry*

O. F. Egginton Company,
Corning, New York, 1899-1920

Oliver Egginton worked as a manager for T. G. Hawkes in 1893; from 1895 to 1899, he was a partner with Walter E. and Walter F. Egginton, former glass cutters for Hawkes. The blanks for the company came from the Corning Glass Works. Patterns found in collections and antique shops include these (Ills. 72 and 73):

Arabian	Creswick
Calvé	Lotus
Cluster	

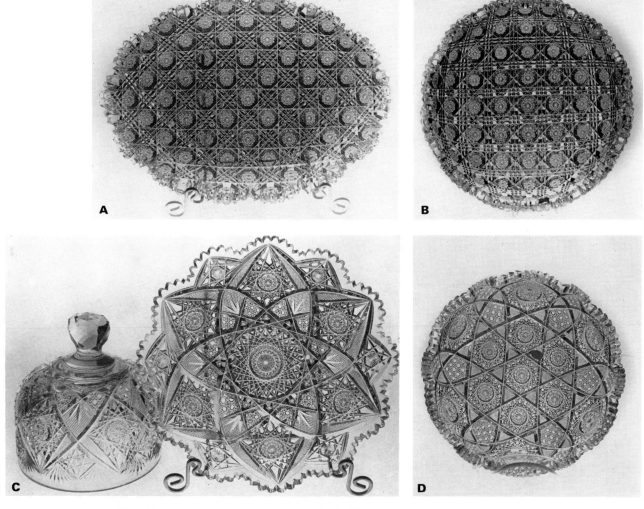

72. Three patterns cut by Egginton. **A.** A 12-inch ice cream tray in Calvé, named for the opera singer Emma Calvé, patented February 4, 1908. Hawkes has the same pattern but called it Imperial. *Patrick Curry.* **B.** A 10-inch signed bowl in Calvé. *Tisnado Collection.* **C.** Signed covered butter in Lotus (7-inch plate, 5-inch dome), patented February 24, 1903. **D.** An 8-inch bowl in Cluster, signed by Egginton (near center). *Roy Brown*

73A. This 7-inch Lotus plate is signed Egginton (marked by black dot). We have seen a bowl in exactly the same pattern signed by Straus. **B.** A signed 8-inch relish tray in Arabian that was identified by Miss Egginton, daughter of O. F. Egginton. **C.** Creswick ice bucket, 8 inches high, was also identified by Miss Egginton. *Tisnado Collection*

56 *Empire Cut Glass Company,*

New York City, ca. 1895-1925

Harry Hollis of Boston founded this company but sold it to his employees, who operated it as a cooperative. In 1902, H. C. Fry bought the company and moved it to Flemington, New Jersey. Louis Iorio created many of the company's designs. We found two patterns—Atlantic and Nelson—in private collections (Ill. 74).

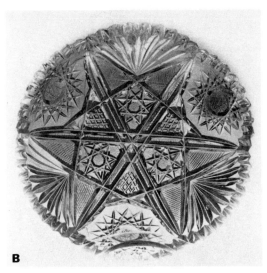

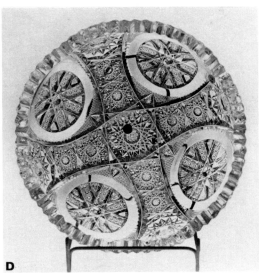

74. An old catalog of the Empire Cut Glass Company provides the identification for (**A**) a 12-inch turkey platter in Atlantic pattern and (**B**) an 8-inch bowl in Nelson. **C.** Two views of a supreme signed Fry on the foot. **D.** A 6-inch bowl also has the Fry signature (marked by dot on the inside center); it is one of Fry's better pieces.

H. C. Fry Glass Company,

Rochester, Pennsylvania, 1901-1934

In 1872 H. C. Fry became president of the Rochester Tumbler Company. This company took the name of H. C. Fry Glass Company in 1901. In 1925 and again in 1933 the firm reorganized; it finally closed in 1934. Fry produced some of the finest lead blanks, but later turned to using cheap figured blanks. Every collector has a piece or two of signed Fry glass, but factory names for the patterns remain undiscovered (Ill. 74).

T. G. Hawkes & Company,
Corning, New York, 1880-1964

Thomas Gibbon Hawkes, a graduate civil engineer, immigrated from Ireland and followed the glass trade of his family, which had long been associated with glassmaking in Waterford, Ireland. He worked as superintendent at Hoare & Dailey Cut Glass Shop until he formed his own company in 1880. Hawkes bought blanks from Corning Glass Works until 1903, when he, Frederick Carder, and Townsend de M. Hawkes formed the Steuben Glass Works. Samuel Hawkes carried on after his father's death in 1913. Since Hawkes produced a large amount of glass, we have been able to find a number of items in these patterns (Ills. 1, 16, 69, 75-81, 106, 110, 175, 214):

Aberdeen	Gravic Chrysanthemum
Brazilian	Gravic Iris
Brunswick	Middlesex
Cardinal	Nautilus
Chrysanthemum	Navarre
Devonshire	Nelson
Fancy Prism	Panel
Festoon	Queens
Gladys	Satin Chrysanthemum
Glencoe	Strawberry-Diamond & Fan
Grecian	Venetian

75. Three pieces that clearly illustrate the skills of Hawkes. **A.** A 6-inch cruet in Venetian, patented June 3, 1890. *David Seiling.* **B.** Tobacco humidor, 8 inches high, in Brunswick. *Doris Patterson.* **C.** Decanter in Chrysanthemum with a silver hinged top.

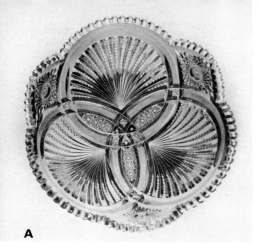

A

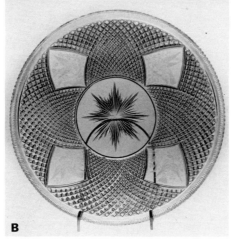

B

C

76. Four well-known patterns by Hawkes. **A.** Inside view of a large punch bowl in Nautilus, patented August 18, 1896. *Tisnado Collection.* **B.** An 11-inch plate in Cardinal, signed in the center. *George Clark.* **C.** Covered cheese dish in Aberdeen, patented April 14, 1896. *Tisnado Collection.* **D.** A 13-inch tray in Venetian, patented June 3, 1890. *George Clark*

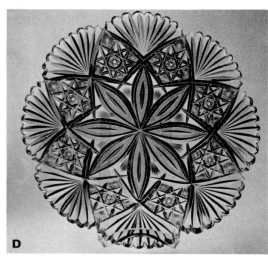

D

77. The champagne glass (**A**) in Brazilian pattern, patented May 28, 1889, was cut for President Diaz of Mexico. *Hebel Collection.* **B.** This pattern was patented by Hawkes on January 25, 1887, and named Middlesex. *Patrick Curry.* **C.** The liqueur bottle is in Glencoe pattern, identified from a Hawkes catalog for 1890. Both the bottle and stopper are signed. *George Clark.* **D.** Pedestal rose globe, 6½ inches tall and signed, is in Brunswick pattern. *Rita Klyce*

A

B

C

D

A

B

78A. The water carafe is Hawkes's Devonshire pattern. *Mrs. Jack Pelzner.* **B.** A 12-inch vase in Brunswick pattern. *Hebel Collection*

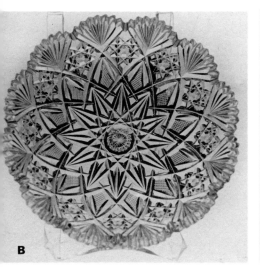

A

79. Three bowls illustrating three patterns, plus a variant, by Hawkes. **A.** A later Panel pattern on a 7-inch signed oblong bowl. *Tisnado Collection.* **B.** A signed 7-inch bowl in Gladys, identified by a Hawkes catalog for 1890. *Mrs. Jack Pelzner.* **C.** The 6-inch bowl is Festoon pattern, patented March 9, 1896. *George Clark.* **D.** The original Panel pattern, patented August 3, 1909; there is a signature in the center of the piece. *George Clark*

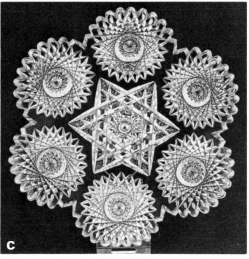

B

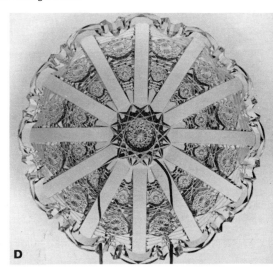

D

80. The large compote in Queens pattern **(A)** is signed Hawkes. It strongly resembles the Queens pattern of Hoare **(83B).** Hawkes used thumbprints and hobstar enclosed in a diamond. Hoare uses the thumbprint, but he alternates the hobstar enclosed in a diamond with cane in a diamond. Gundy-Clapperton (Canada) cut a similar pattern **(159A).** *Rita Klyce.* **B.** The tumbler in Gravic Iris is one of the last patterns cut by Hawkes.

A

B

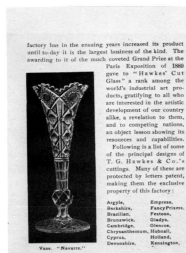

81. A page from the Hawkes book, circa 1890, listing patterns and illustrating Navarre. *First California Regional Group National Early American Glass Club.* The footed rose globe is in Iris pattern. A statement on the photograph, which was folded when mailed to Mrs. Jack Walker by a Hawkes relative, claims this was the last pattern cut by the company.

J. Hoare & Company,

Corning, New York, 1853-1920

John Hoare apprenticed under his father, James Hoare, in Cork, Ireland, then worked for various English companies, including Thomas Webb & Sons, before immigrating to Philadelphia in 1853. He and five partners founded a cutting shop. He bought out all but one partner and formed Hoare & Burns two years later. Then he bought the cutting shop of the Brooklyn Flint Glass Company and called it Gould & Hoare and later Hoare and Dailey. In 1868, he became associated with the Corning Flint Glass Company, but he retained the cut glass department under the name of J. Hoare and Company. Some collectors we know own pieces in these patterns (Ills. 45, 82-83, 150, 189):

Creswick   Nassau
Florence   Queens
Hindoo   Wheat
Monarch

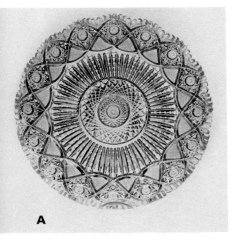

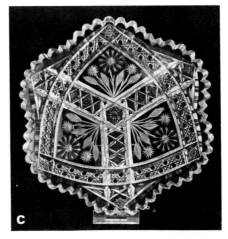

82. Four well-known patterns cut by Hoare. **A.** 14-inch tray in Creswick. **B.** 4-inch sachet jar in Hindoo pattern. **C.** 7-inch plate in Nassau. *Jean Rieth.* **D.** 6-inch-high bell in Monarch pattern. *Patrick Curry*

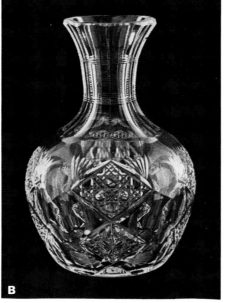

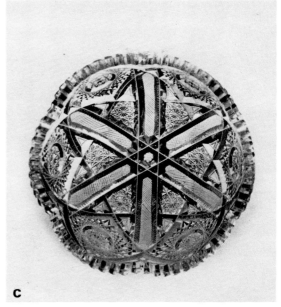

83. The hinged handkerchief box in Nassau pattern (**A**) is very rare; the silver is signed by Birks. **B.** Signed Hoare water carafe in Queens. **C.** We have seen a bowl like this one in two collections. It is Florence pattern, patented by George L. Abbott on February 15, 1887. The bowl shown here has a feather between the miters, but the other one has crosshatching. *Walker Collection* and *Thelma Prouse.* **D.** A butter tub signed Hobbs Gold Medal. *George Clark*

Hobbs Glass Company,

Wheeling, West Virginia, 1845-1891

In 1845, John L. Hobbs and James B. Barnes took over Excelsior Glass Works and called it Hobbs, Barnes & Company. The company reorganized in 1863 as Hobbs, Brockunier & Company. Eventually it became Hobbs Glass Company, which joined the United States Glass Company in 1891. We have found one signed piece from this company but no pattern names (Ill. 83).

Hope Glass Works,

Providence, Rhode Island, 1872-1951

Martin L. Kern organized the company, and his son took it over in 1891. John R. de Goey and his brother bought the company in 1899, and continued using the name until 1951, when W. Edmund de Goey liquidated the company. We found two pieces of cut glass in an antique shop with the signature of this company (Ill. 84).

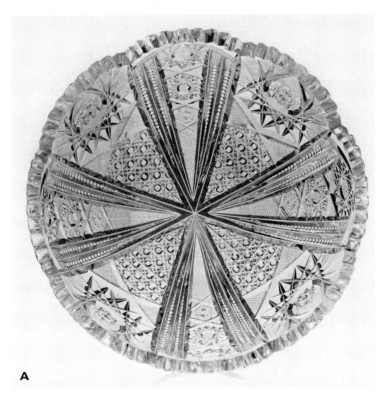

A

B

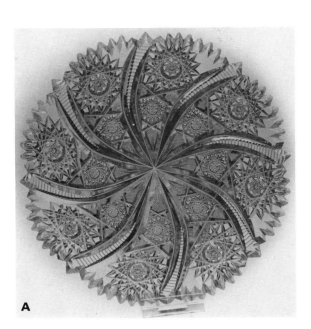

A

C

84. An inside view (**A**) of a bowl signed by the Hope Glass Works. **B.** Another bowl of the same size, 9 inches, with the same signature. *Wardlow Collection.* **C.** An oddly shaped nappy with a top handle, in Royal pattern by Hunt, patented July 11, 1911.

85A. A 7-inch plate is signed by the Laurel Cut Glass Company. *Dorothy Herrington.* **B & C.** Two pieces in patterns by Irving: a signed 9-inch boat in Iowa and a 10-inch plate in Victrola (according to an old Irving catalog). *Tisnado Collection*

C

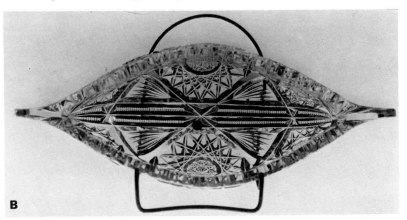

B

Hunt Glass Company,

Corning, New York, 1895-?

Thomas Hunt and his son Harry immigrated to the United States in 1880 from England and settled in White Mills. When Thomas died, his son took over the business. The company at first used blanks from Corning Glass Works, but later bought pressed blanks from Union Glass Company. We have found many pieces in Royal pattern, patented July 11, 1911 (Ills. 53, 84).

Irving Cut Glass Company, Inc.,

Honesdale, Pennsylvania, 1900-1930

Six men formed this corporation in 1900. One of them, William H. Hawken, became the firm's designer. The company worked on figured blanks purchased from Fry. They conducted extensive business with South Africa, Spain, China, and Japan. We have two catalog patterns signed "Irving" (Ills. 67, 85):

"Corinthian"	Victrola
Iowa	

Jewel Cut Glass Company,

Newark, New Jersey, 1906-1928

The company originally took the name of C. H. Taylor Glass Company, but in 1907 this was changed to Jewel Cut Glass Company. Henry L. Luckock worked as the factory foreman and designer. One collector we know has a piece in Aberdeen pattern (Ill. 86).

86A. A 6-inch caviar jar by Krantz-Smith & Company. *George Clark.* **B.** A 16-inch plate in Aberdeen by Jewel Cut Glass Company, patented March 19, 1912. *Tisnado Collection.* **C.** A 4½-inch cereal pitcher in Silver Thread cut by William Marrett for Libbey, patented January 15, 1901. *C. W. Moody*

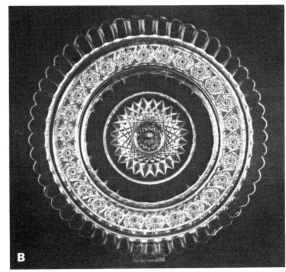

64 *Krantz-Smith & Company,*

Honesdale, Pennsylvania, 1893-1932

John E. Krantz and John H. Smith operated a cutting shop and established showrooms in Chicago and New York City. In 1899, George W. Sell joined the firm. Krantz sold his interest to Sell in 1920, and the company then went under the name of G. Sell & Company. In 1932, a fire destroyed the factory. One collector showed us a piece from this company (Ill. 86).

Emil F. Kupfer, Inc.,

Brooklyn, New York, 1912-1929

Emil. F. Kupfer, a cutter, started this corporation. Francis R. Smith assigned one half of the "Good Luck" pattern to Kupfer in July 29, 1913 (Ill. 87).

Lackawanna Cut Glass Company,

Scranton, Pennsylvania, 1903-1905

This company sold cut glass products by mail directly to the consumer, on a money-back guarantee if not satisfied. It cut more than 90 patterns, but we have seen only a signed water carafe and a tumbler (Ill. 87).

Laurel Cut Glass Company,

Jermyn, Pennsylvania, 1903-1920

Originally started as the German Cut Glass Company in 1903, this firm soon took the name of Laurel Cut Glass Company. In 1906, it changed to Kohinur Cut Glass Company, but in 1907 it reassumed the Laurel name. Shortly before it went out of business in 1920, the firm became associated with the Cut Glass Corporation of America (Quaker Cut Glass Company). The company used women as polishers and cutters of simple designs. We have seen a plate with the Laurel signature in one collection (Ill. 85).

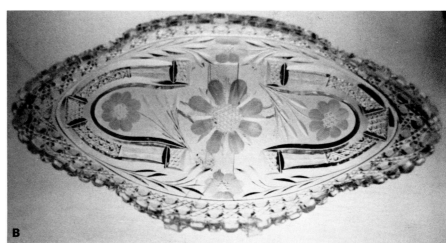

87. The water carafe (**A**) is a rare one, signed by Lackawanna Cut Glass Company. We have seen two tumblers with the same signature. *Walker Collection.* **B.** The "Horseshoe," or "Good Luck," tray was cut by Francis R. Smith for Emil F. Kupfer, Inc., patented July 29, 1913; it shows the predominance of flower decoration at that time. *Tisnado Collection*

Libbey Glass Company,
Toledo, Ohio, 1888-1936

William L. Libbey joined the New England Glass company staff in 1872. Edward Drummond Libbey joined his father in the dissolution of the New England Glass Company in 1874. In 1888, the company incorporated under the name of W. L. Libbey & Sons, when the factory moved to Toledo, Ohio. The firm officially took the name of Libbey Glass Company in 1892. In 1936 it became a part of the Owens-Illinois Glass Company.

Cutters for the company included George E. Hatch, William C. Anderson, Solon O. Richardson, Jr., William Marrett, and Dennis Spillane. Libbey and Hawkes produced, between them, a large percentage of the cut glass made in the United States and supplied blanks to many smaller companies as well; consequently, we have found many catalog patterns for Libbey (Ills. 13, 44, 86, 88-95, 220):

Corinthian	New Brilliant
Delphos	Ozella
Elsmere	Prism
Empress	Princess
Eulalia	Rajah
Florence	Senora
Glenda	Silver Thread
Gloria	Spillane
Harvard	Star & Feather
Jewel	Sultana
Imperial	Sunset
Iola	Waverly
Kingston	No. 100
Libbey	

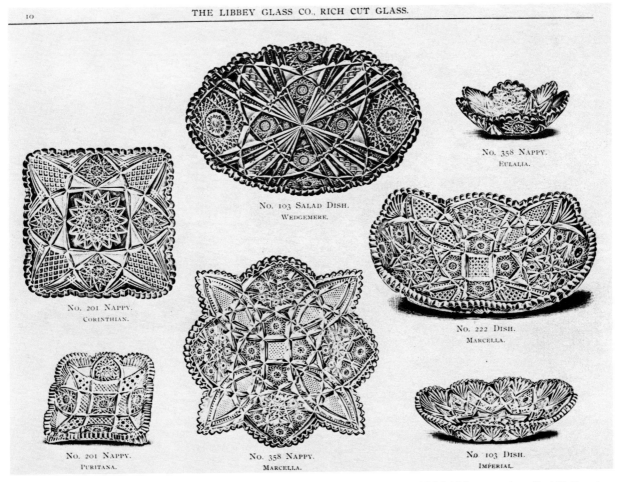

10   THE LIBBEY GLASS CO., RICH CUT GLASS.

No. 103 Salad Dish.
WEDGEMERE.

No. 358 Nappy.
EULALIA.

No. 201 Nappy.
CORINTHIAN.

No. 222 Dish.
MARCELLA.

No. 358 Nappy.
MARCELLA.

No. 201 Nappy.
PURITANA.

No. 103 Dish.
IMPERIAL.

88. A page from the 1896 Libbey catalog. *Carl U. Fauster*

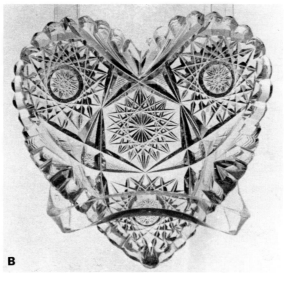

A

B

C

89. Three patterns identified from Libbey catalogs. **A.** A 6-inch-high spooner in Sultana, patented January 15, 1901, identified by a 1900-1910 catalog. **B.** Heart-shaped nappy cut in the same pattern. *Walker Collection.* **C.** Champagne glass in Imperial signed Libbey, patented June 4, 1895, identified from the 1896 catalog. *Patrick Curry.* **D.** Two water goblets; the one at left is signed Averbeck and Almy and Thomas; the one at right in Princess pattern, patented July 21, 1894, is signed Libbey. It was identified by an 1896 catalog. *Walker Collection*

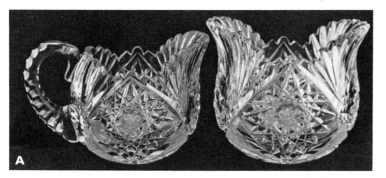

A

D

B

90A. Sugar and creamer in Eulalia, shown in an 1896 Libbey catalog. *Aubright Collection.* **B.** Punch cup signed Libbey is in Waverly pattern, identified in the 1900-1910 catalog; the one at right is signed Hawkes. *Argie Burwell.* **C.** A set of glasses for sherry, wine, champagne, and water in Jewel is signed by Libbey with two different signatures. Jewel was identified in the 1904 Libbey catalog.

C

A

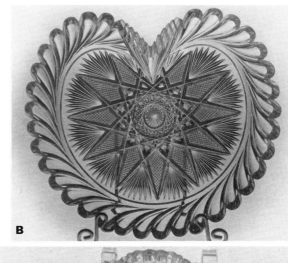

B

91A. A 10-inch tray in Senora signed Libbey that was shown in the 1904 catalog. *George Clark.* **B.** Heart-shaped tray in Florence Star, signed Libbey, which was patented April 23, 1889 and is listed in the 1893 catalog. Libbey named the pattern for his bride. *Hebel Collection.* **C.** The 8-inch double-handled bowl signed Libbey is in a pattern called Sunset, which was shown in the 1904 Libbey catalog. *Walker Collection*

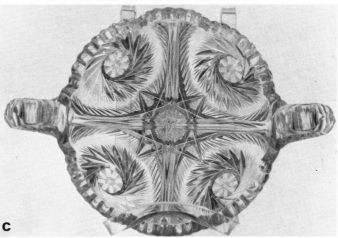

C

92. Most of these patterns appear in various Libbey catalogs. **A.** An 8-inch signed bowl in Corinthian, patented June 2, 1896, and shown in the 1896 catalog. *Patrick Curry.* **B.** A 10-inch plate in Kingston, identified by the 1904 catalog; signed Libbey near the rim. **C.** A 7-inch plate signed Libbey; pattern was patented by D. F. Spillane on May 8, 1906, and referred to as Spillane. *Patrick Curry* and *Hebel Collection.* **D.** This 8 ½-inch compote in Ozella is identified by the 1909 catalog. *Rita Klyce.* **E.** Signed covered butter dish in Rajah pattern, which appeared in the 1904 catalog. *George Clark.* **F.** A 14-inch shallow bowl in Libbey pattern, shown in the 1909 catalog.

B

C

D

E

F

93. Four more patterns produced by Libbey. **A.** Signed 8-inch bowl; pattern was patented March 13, 1899, by William Marrett and listed as #100 in catalog. **B.** An 8-inch bowl in Star and Feather, patented May 8, 1906, by William C. Anderson and assigned to Libbey; shown in the 1909 catalog. *Roy Brown.* **C.** Signed 8-inch plate in Gloria. **D.** Delphos pattern 8-inch bowl is a signed Libbey piece. *George Clark*

94. Two patterns from the 1900 Libbey catalog. **A.** Footed bowl in Prism signed Libbey. *Tisnado Collection.* **B.** A 9-inch bowl in Glenda, signed Libbey. *Marie Hegarty*

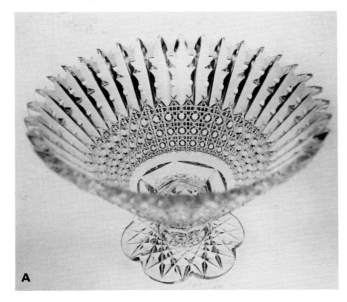

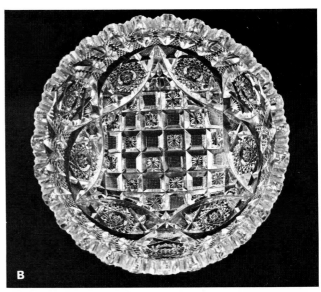

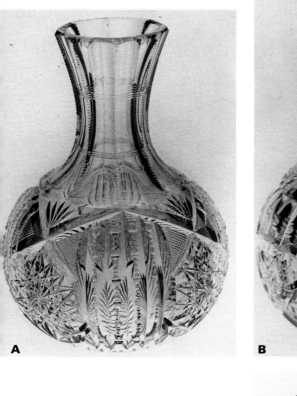

A

B

C

D

95A. This water carafe is identified as New Brilliant pattern in the 1908 Libbey catalog. *Adolph F. Hansen and Patrick Curry.* **B.** A carafe in Elsmere pattern, signed on the flute, that appeared in the 1900 catalog. **C.** Milk pitcher in Harvard pattern that appeared in the 1893 catalog. *George Clark.* **D.** The signed 11 ½-inch champagne pitcher is in Iola pattern, from the 1909 catalog. *Hebel Collection*

Lyons Cut Glass Company,
Lyons, New York, 1903-1905

This company organized in 1903 with James Bashford as president. The blanks for cutting came from Union Glass Works in Somerville, Massachusetts, and from Fry, Baccarat, and others. N. J. Ewer & Sons of Youngstown, Ohio, bought the stock on hand in 1905. We have seen one signed piece made by this company.

70 *Majestic Cut Glass Company,*

Elmira, New York, 1900-ca. 1916

Wolf M. Spiegel and his son Saul organized this company. A dealer showed us a nappy signed with an "M" in a circle.

Maple City Glass Company,

Hawley, Pennsylvania, ca. 1910-?

John S. O'Connor owned this firm. It operated long enough to publish 10 illustrated catalogs. We own a pair of matching lifeboats with the company signature (Ill. 96).

96A. Celery in the shape of a lifeboat, signed inside with the maple leaf of the Maple City Glass Company. **B.** Two-handled spooner signed Libbey on flat of the handle. *Tisnado Collection.* **C.** An 8-inch-high compote in Meriden catalog pattern #136. *C. W. Moody*

Meriden Cut Glass Company,
Meriden, Connecticut, 1895-1923

In 1898, this firm joined with a number of smaller ones to form the International Silver Company. The Meriden Silver Plate Company was organized in 1870; in 1895 a subsidiary, the Meriden Cut Glass Company, was started to cut tableware. After it became part of International Silver Company, it continued in operation until 1923. Thomas A. Shaley, the foreman, applied for patents on designs between 1904 and 1918, which he assigned to the parent corporation. Several collectors have showed us the following patterns (Ills. 96-98):

Alhambra or Greek Key	No. 136
Plymouth	No. 227 F

97. Two patterns shown in the Meriden Cut Glass Company catalog and one Mt. Washington piece. **A.** A covered cheese dish in Plymouth. **B.** A 7-inch plate in a pattern identified as #227F. **C.** A 7-inch plate in a pattern patented by Thomas Singleton on January 31, 1893, for Mt. Washington Glass Company. *Jean Rieth*

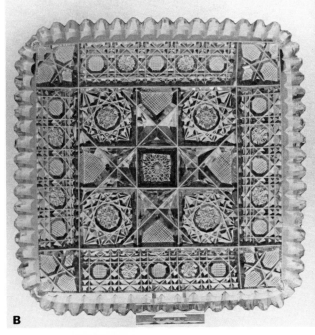

98. Four difficult-to-find bottles. **A.** A Meriden 9 ½-inch vinegar cruet in Alhambra. **B.** A Worcestershire bottle, 8 inches, in Alhambra pattern. **C.** A 6-inch green decanter in Wheeler pattern by Mt. Washington. *C. W. Moody*. **D.** Matching decanters in Plymouth, identified from Meriden catalog. *George Clark*

Mt. Washington Glass Company,

73

New Bedford, Massachusetts, 1837-1894

Deming Jarves, agent of the Boston & Sandwich Glass Company, started this firm in South Boston in 1837 as the Mt. Washington Glass Works. The factory closed early in 1860. Later in that same year, Timothy Howe and W. L. Libbey rented the facilities and continued to operate the company under the name of Mt. Washington Glass Works. When Howe died in 1866, Libbey purchased the company. In 1869, he took over a more modern plant of the now bankrupt New Bedford Glass Company and transferred the Mt. Washington Glass Works to this new facility. Finally, in 1871, a stock company called Mt. Washington Glass Company was formed with W. L. Libbey as agent and Captain Henry Libbey as superintendent. W. L. Libbey resigned in 1872, to become agent for the New England Glass Company in Boston. Captain Libbey resigned in 1874, and the company closed in 1874 but reopened in 1876. In 1880, the company organized the Pairpoint Manufacturing Company to produce both staple and fancy plated silver articles. The Pairpoint Corporation absorbed the Mt. Washington Glass Company in 1894. Patterns identified by collectors include (Ills. 97-99, 150):

Albert Steffin (patented October 27, 1908)   Thomas Singleton (patented January 31, 1893)
Radiant   Wheeler

99A. Dresser tray, patented by Albert Steffin for Mt. Washington Glass Company on October 27, 1909, is in a pattern known as "Tulip." **B.** A 10-inch bowl in Princess by John S. O'Connor, patented February 19, 1895. *Mrs. Jack Pelzner.* **C.** "Palm Leaf Fan" cut by Thomas Singleton for the Ohio Cut Glass Company, patented April 5, 1904. *Walker Collection.* **D.** An 8-inch water pitcher in Radiant pattern by Mt. Washington.

74 *John S. O'Connor,*

Hawley, Pennsylvania, 1890-1900
Goshen, Pennsylvania, 1900-1919

John S. O'Connor, who had formerly worked for Dorflinger, opened a factory in Hawley, Pennsylvania, in 1890 and sold it to the Maple City Glass Company in 1900. He then opened another factory in Goshen, Pennsylvania, in 1900. From 1902 to 1904, he operated the American Cut Glass Company in Port Jervis, New York, with his son, Arthur E. O'Connor, in charge. He bought blanks from Dorflinger. One collection we photographed contained an item in Princess pattern (patented February 19, 1895) (Ill. 99).

Ohio Cut Glass Company,

Bowling Green, Ohio, ?-1912

This company operated as a cutting shop for Pitkin and Brooks. Thomas Singleton became manager; he designed Palm Leaf pattern, April 5, 1904 (Ill. 99). The shop burned in 1912.

Pairpoint Corporation,

New Bedford, Massachusetts, 1880-1938

In 1880, Mt. Washington Glass Company organized the Pairpoint Manufacturing Company to produce silver-plated items. The subsidiary took over the parent firm and changed the name to Pairpoint Corporation. One collector of our acquaintance owns colored-cut-to-clear glass in Adelaide and Lincoln patterns. Another has a 16-inch plate in Coronal pattern by Pairpoint. We photographed pieces in the following patterns (Ills. 4, 15, 100):

Avila   Viscaria
Russian

100A. This 10-inch compote by Pairpoint, with teardrop and hobstar base, is in Avila pattern. *Ardene Fairchild Smith.* **B.** A 10-inch triangular dish in Russian pattern by Pairpoint that appears in inventory photographs.

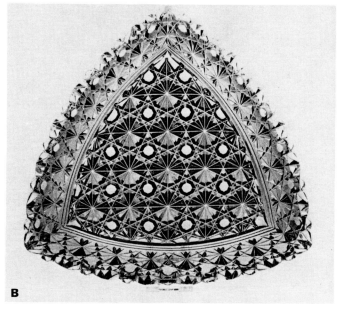

Pitkin & Brooks,

Chicago, Illinois, 1872-ca. 1920

Edward Hand Pitkin and Jonathan William Brooks owned this firm that made both blanks and cut glass. Some of their blanks were sent to Europe for cutters there to use in producing Pitkin and Brooks patterns. This firm became the largest wholesale distributor of glassware and crockery in the Midwest. We have found the following catalog pieces in various collections (Ills. 101-104):

Athole	Myrtle
Belmont	Osborn
Border	Plymouth
Cleo	Rajah
Heart	

101. A page from the Pitkin & Brooks catalog, circa 1907. *Kitty and Russell Umbraco*

76

102. A page from the Pitkin & Brooks catalog, 1907. *Kitty and Russell Umbraco*

103. Six patterns identified by the 1907 Pitkin & Brooks catalog. **A.** An 8-inch shallow bowl in Belmont. *Alice Peri.* **B.** Heavily cut 8-inch bowl in Athole pattern. *Marie Hegarty.*

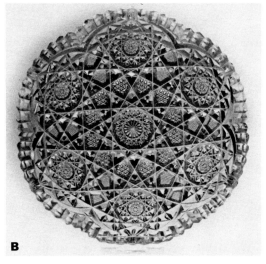

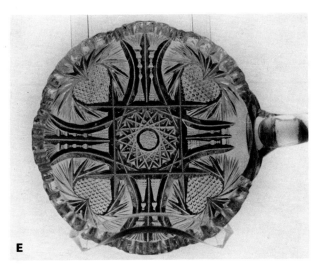

103C. A 7-inch relish tray in Osborn. *Patrick Curry.* **D.** An 8-inch bowl in Plymouth. **E.** A 6-inch nappy in Heart. *Ann Dunlap.* **F.** An 8-inch bowl in Cleo, but it has a Fry signature. *Hunt Collection*

Quaker City Cut Glass Company,
Philadelphia, Pennsylvania, 1902-1927

This glass company, first listed in 1902 in the city directory, was also known under the name of Cut Glass Corporation of America. In 1907 Thomas Wolstenholme became president. The company moved to Jermyn, Pennsylvania, in 1924. After World War I it had joined with the Laurel Cut Glass Company, but the two separated a short time later and Quaker City returned to its old location in Philadelphia. The company identified its wares with gummed labels showing a bust of William Penn. We have seen only one piece identified by catalog, Empress pattern (Ill. 166).

104. Three patterns by Pitkin and Brooks, as identified from a 1904-1905 catalog: **A.** A 10-inch tray in Myrtle with a hobstar center. *Hunt Collection.* **B.** A 7-inch compote in Border pattern. *Hebel Collection.* **C.** Sugar and creamer in Rajah pattern. *C. W. Moody.* All pieces are signed.

H. P. Sinclaire & Company,
Corning, New York, 1904-1929

H. P. Sinclaire, a former partner of Hawkes, organized this company and served as the designer. He used Dorflinger blanks because he considered them the best on the market. Sinclaire favored engraving over heavy cutting. Collectors who like engraving have found these patterns (Ills. 18, 40, 105-106):

Adam	Flute and Panel Border (April 5, 1910)
Apples, Grapes and Pears	Queens
Baronial	Westminster
Bengal	No. 1023

Sterling Cut Glass Company,
Cincinnati, Ohio, ca. 1904-1950

Joseph Phillips and Joseph Landenwitsch headed this company. We have seen two signed pieces of this firm's cut glass, one with a script "Sterling" and one with "Sterling" block printed. Later Phillips worked as a salesman for the Rookwood Pottery Company. One collection includes a piece in Arcadia pattern (Ill. 107).

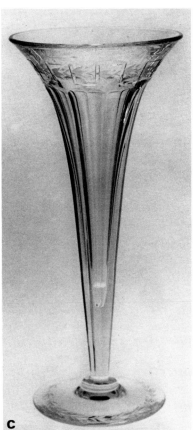

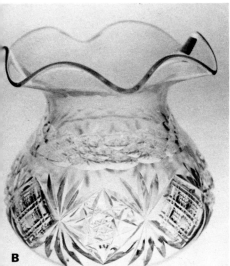

105. Four patterns by Sinclaire. **A.** Signed whiskey jug, 5 inches tall, in Bengal. *Hebel Collection.* **B.** Flower center in Baronial signed Sinclaire. *Tisnado Collection.* **C.** An 11-inch vase in Flute and Panel Border, patented April 5, 1910. **D.** Signed whiskey decanter in Queens. *Hebel Collection*

106. Two signed pitchers make an interesting contrast. **A.** This 7-inch pitcher in Westminster is signed by Sinclaire. *Irma Adams.* **B.** Pitcher, signed by Hawkes, in Brunswick pattern. **C.** Adam pattern 12-inch tray with Sinclaire signature.

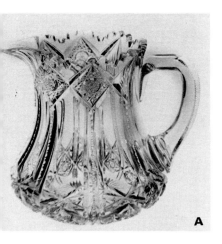

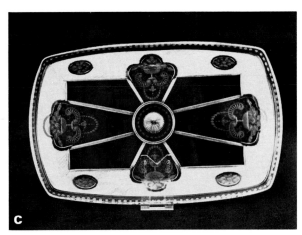

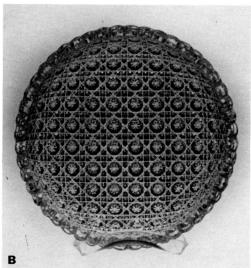

107. Two patterns by Sterling Cut Glass Company. **A.** Covered butter dish in Arcadia. **B.** Signed 8-inch bowl with a pyramidal star covering the button. *C. W. Moody*

L. Straus & Sons,
New York City, 1888-?

Lazarus Straus came to the United States from Bavaria and worked as a salesman for a china and glassware import company. He organized his own firm and began cutting glass in 1888. His Corinthian pattern closely resembles a pattern of the same name done by Libbey (Ill. 108).

Taylor Brothers,
Philadelphia, Pennsylvania, 1902-1915

In 1902, Albert Taylor, his brother Lafayette, and John H. Williams formed Taylor Brothers & Williams. By 1904 the name had become Taylor Brothers. The company filed for bankruptcy in 1911 and went out of business in 1915. We have photographed a number of items signed "Taylor Brothers" but have discovered no catalog names (Ill. 109).

Tuthill Cut Glass Company,
Middletown, New York, 1900-1923

Charles G. Tuthill joined with James F. and Susan Tuthill to establish this company. Charles Tuthill created most of the designs and became famous for his intaglio cut. A collector of intaglio owns pieces in two catalog patterns, Wild Rose and Primrose (Ill. 110).

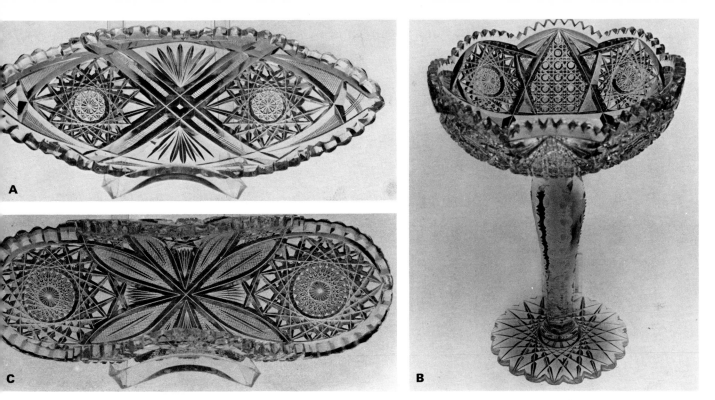

108. Three pieces by Straus. **A.** Signed 11-inch celery tray. *Roy Brown.* **B.** A 12-inch compote in Corinthian. *Lucinda Baker Greiner.* **C.** Signed 10-inch spoon tray with split vesicas. *Walker Collection*

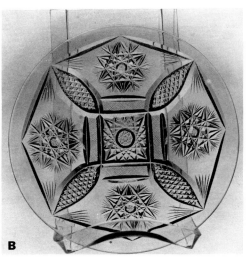

109A&B. An 8-inch bowl and a 6-inch plate, both signed Unger Brothers. **C.** This 7-inch plate has a rare signature, Van Heusen. **D.** Taylor Brothers signed this 5-inch nappy. *Walker Collection*

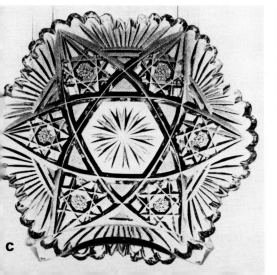

82   *Unger Brothers,*

Newark, New Jersey, 1901-1918

This company cut heavy glass at first then resorted to cheaper pressed blanks. We have found one particular pattern most plentiful but have no catalog name for it (Ill. 109).

Union Glass Company,

Somerville, Massachusetts, 1851-1927

Amory Houghton started this firm in 1851. He sold his interest in the company to Julian de Cordova, who expanded the facilities. The company put its initials on the liners of ferneries, urns, and spittoons. We own such a fernery (Ill. 111).

110. These two items show the similarity of intaglio patterns. **A.** The cologne bottle with sterling silver top is Wild Rose pattern, signed Tuthill. **B.** The hinged powder box is Hawkes's Satin Chrysanthemum signed on the inside lid. *Tisnado Collection*

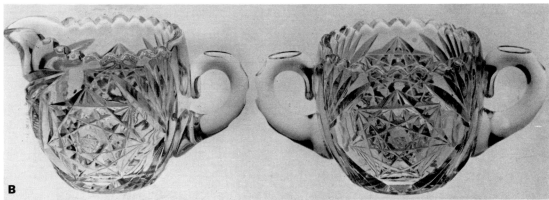

111A. The sugar and creamer here have Wright on the flat of the handles. *Roy Brown*. **B.** This set has the Wright signature on the flat of the handle and on the base. **C.** The lining of the fernery, 7 inches in diameter, is marked UGCO Somerville. **D.** A 12-inch celery tray cut by Western Cut Glass Company.

84
Van Heusen, Charles Company,
Albany, New York, 1893-?

This firm served as an agent for Libbey Glass Company, but it also bought products from several small cutting shops and etched its signature on them. We saw such a piece in one collection (Ill. 109).

Western Cut Glass Company,
Chicago, Illinois, 1914-1918

Herman and Frank Kotwitz, with Harry Baumann, organized the Western Cut Glass Company. The firm sold to Marshall Field & Company in Chicago. One collector showed us a piece made by this company (Ill. 111).

Wright Rich Cut Glass Company,
Anderson, Indiana, 1904-1915

George W. Wright served as president and Thomas W. Wright as treasurer. A number of collectors have owned pieces of signed Wright glass (Ill. 111).

The names of patterns disappear with time and the vanishing of old catalogs, but a signature offers a more permanent means of identification—at least of the company that manufactured a piece. As the cut glass industry expanded in the United States, competition greatly increased. One result of this competitive situation was a more extensive use of signatures.

5.

IDENTIFICATION
BY SIGNATURE

WHEN RENEWED INTEREST IN CUT GLASS DEVELOPED, COLLECTORS AND dealers suddenly wanted to know more about this type of glass. Everyone soon learned that a signature offered one positive means of identifying the company that produced the glass, and the ensuing rush to find signed pieces often inflated their value.

History of Signatures

We have heard some people explain, "Of course, this piece isn't signed—it was cut long before they used signatures." The fact is that no one can say positively when signatures first appeared on cut glass. On some pieces one does not expect to find a signature because the company produced them in the early years of cut glass, but—paradoxically—there is a signature. On other pieces cut with a late pattern, there is no signature, although the knowledgeable collector might expect to find one (Ill. 112).

We can explain only *why* this glass was signed: the manufacturer wanted to protect his patterns and the reputation of his company. This desire eventually brought about the extensive use of signatures, but a patent supposedly offered the same protection.

112. These two signed trays show the distinctive characteristics of the glasshouse, and so they need no signature—except for positive identification. **A.** 12-inch bread tray signed Pitkin & Brooks. *Roy Brown.* **B.** 10-inch tray signed Hawkes. *George Clark*

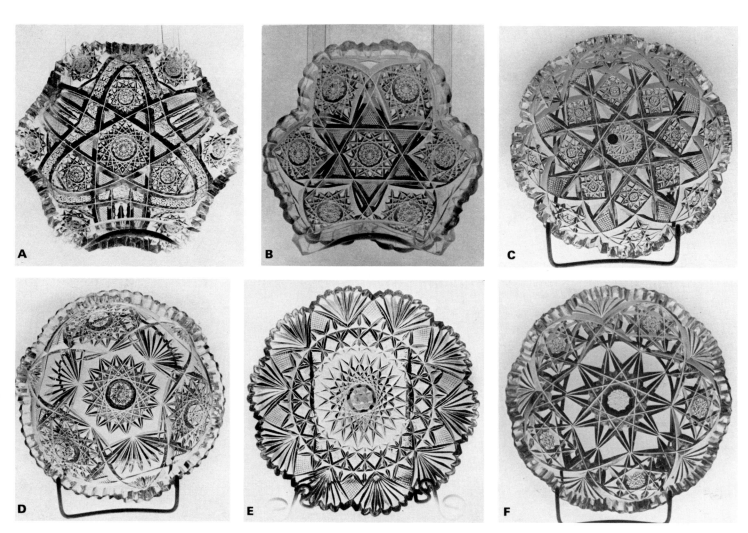

113. Six signed pieces that are decorated with the same motifs in slightly different arrangements; they vary in size from 5 to 7 inches. **A.** Bowl signed by Hoare. *Walker Collection.* **B.** This small nappy signed Egginton strongly resembles his Lotus pattern and also the Hoare bowl in **A.** *Walker Collection.* **C.** Four collectors have this nappy signed Hawkes (at the dot) that resembles his Brazilian pattern. **D.** This nappy signed Clark uses the same motifs as the Hawkes one, but in larger size. *Mrs. Jack Pelzner.* **E.** Plate signed Hoare has little in common with the Hoare piece in **A.** *Hebel Collection.* **F.** A bowl signed Sinclaire looks more like a Hawkes piece with the 8-point star. *Roy Brown*

Patents

When a master cutter designed a unique pattern, the glasshouse for which he worked usually obtained a patent in his name. Then he automatically assigned the pattern to the company. The patent covered varying periods of time: three and one-half, seven, or fourteen years. When it expired, the design went into the public domain.

As cut glass grew in popularity, numerous small cutting shops sprang up—literally—in barns, sheds, or on the back porches of houses. Some lasted only a short time before going broke or selling out to another cutting shop. "The competition in the glass business was so great," William Wixson reported, "they cut each other's throats faster than they cut glass." (Ill. 113.)

Small shops could not afford patternmakers, nor could many of the owners themselves create designs. Therefore, to meet the competition, both small and the large shops very often managed to "break" the patents of popular patterns. The fact that a pattern contained a dominant and several minor motifs simplified patent breaking. By changing a minor motif, perhaps substituting a strawberry diamond for crosshatching on the original, the cutter avoided actually infringing on a patent (Ill. 114). This slight change in pattern went unnoticed by the casual buyer, who chose an item for its eye appeal rather than by company.

A

B

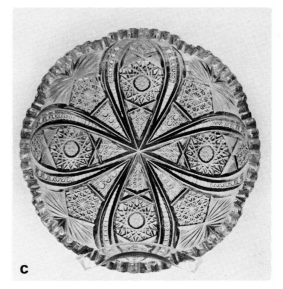

C

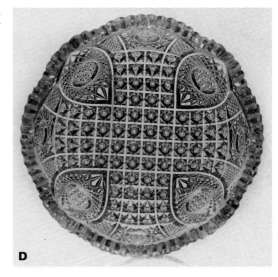

D

114A. This 9-inch bowl signed Clark strongly resembles the pattern of the 8-inch bowl (**B**) signed Hoare. *Walker Collection, Thelma Prouse.* **C.** An 8-inch bowl signed Sinclaire (he was once Hawkes's partner) has the general design of Chrysanthemum pattern and really looks more like a Hawkes piece than a Sinclaire. **D.** This 8-inch bowl has an Irving signature but resembles the style of Fry. *Aubright Collection*

88

In addition, itinerant cutters who moved from one company to another encouraged the owners to cut familiar or favorite designs with the dominant motifs they knew best. By slight variations, such as changing the number of points in a hobstar or creating a different center for the star, they could easily create a new design (Ill. 115).

William Wixson, who apprenticed under Thomas Singleton, found this designer's patterns easy to change. "While I kept the major interest of the pattern, I would change it enough to keep it legal." Although Wixson never created a pattern, his value to a glasshouse, in addition to his cutting skill and artistry, was his special ability to break the patents of Singleton and other top designers. "I could call any glasshouse, and the owner would pay my expenses to come work for him," Wixson told us proudly.

Often a cutter would take his training with a company and create a number of designs for them, then go into business for himself but not change his creative style. Consequently, the designs he made later would strongly resemble those he had made for his former employer. Compare the work of Hawkes, Egginton, and Sinclaire or that of Dorflinger and O'Connor. Tuthill had a most distinctive style.

Look at the various pieces of cut glass in your own collection. How many times have you thought you had found an exact match for a piece, only to dis-

115. Only a slight variation could change a pattern. **A.** This ice cream tray, 13 inches, signed Egginton, uses crosshatching with the hobstars. **B.** The 6-inch relish signed Hoare uses cane with the hobstar. (The dot, as usual, marks the signature.) *George Clark.* **C.** The 8-inch two-handled bowl with divisions has a Hawkes signature, but it resembles the Chrysanthemum pattern. *Rita Klyce.* **D.** Here a bowl of the same size has the distinctive Tuthill style and signature. *Walker Collection*

116. A cutter never forgot the designs of his former employers. **A.** This 7-inch plate signed Hoare looks a good deal like Hawkes's work. *George Clark.* **B.** A 9-inch bowl signed Sinclaire follows the same basic design as Hawkes's Chrysanthemum. *Irma Adams.* **C.** An 8-inch bowl signed Clark resembles the Sinclaire bowl. *Mrs. Jack Pelzner.* **D.** The heavy cutting of this 10-inch bowl signed Libbey looks more like Pitkin & Brooks's work. *Ardene Fairchild Smith.* **E.** A 10-inch plate signed Libbey has much in common with the plate by Hoare (in **A**). *Walker Collection.* **F.** This 9-inch bowl strongly resembles the work of Egginton although it carries a Hawkes signature. *Roy Brown*

cover one slight variation? Perhaps the patent record or catalog showed a buzz star rather than a hobstar. It was this constant breaking of patents that brought about the more extensive use of signatures.

Pieces Without Signatures

Many pieces cut during the early years of the Brilliant Period have no signatures. Originally, when a piece of glass revealed unusual workmanship, a signature was used to authenticate the artistry of the item—a number of companies signed only their finest or museum pieces (Ill. 118).

A dealer in Missoula, Montana, pointed out to us that Tuthill, in the early years, signed only the outstanding items. She showed us a two-part round box, fourteen inches in diameter, with intaglio cutting of fruits combined with a simple buzz on the lid. On a clear spot between the lid and the buzz design of the lower part, Tuthill had signed with a formalized fish under the name. The dealers suggested that possibly he used this signature only on his finest pieces. We have questioned many dealers and collectors, but very few have seen this signature and neither have we—except on this particular piece.

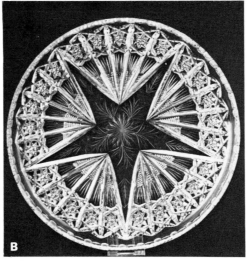
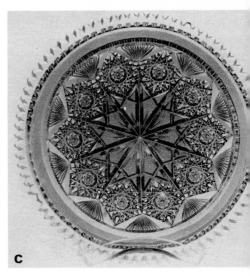

117. These three plates, all signed and 10 inches in diameter, show unusual workmanship. **A.** Plate with the signature of the Maple City Glass Company. *Rita Klyce.* **B.** Plate signed Tuthill that has unusual balance in its design. *Tisnado Collection.* **C.** Heavily cut plate signed Tuthill. *Walker Collection*

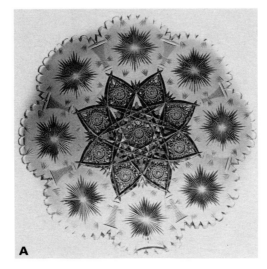

118. Two outstanding pieces by Hawkes: **A.** 15-inch plate signed Hawkes. *C. W. Moody.* **B.** Large flower center in Gladys pattern, with separate sterling silver top marked Shreve. The center weighs 22½ pounds, is 15½ inches high and 14 inches in diameter. The photograph by Mike de la Cruz was taken at a lecture. *Dorothy Murphy*

From time to time glass companies made pieces for presentation to outstanding individuals; these were sometimes signed, sometimes not. A pair of bowling pin decanters, obviously presentation pieces, bears the Libbey signature. We own a small nappy that carries both the Libbey signature with a sword and another with a crescent overlaid with a scimitar, probably the emblem of a lodge or fraternal organization. We have never seen this signature on any other piece of cut glass (Ill. 119).

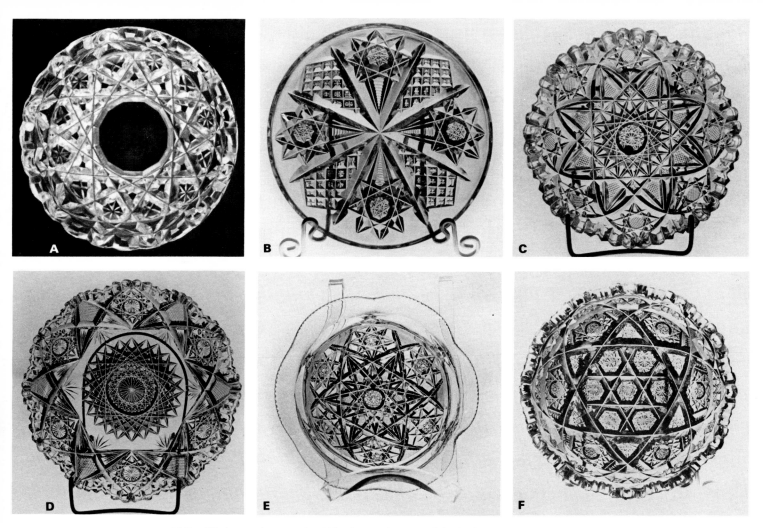

119. All these pieces—the 5-inch nappies and 6-inch plates—have signatures, but the pieces vary in quality. **A.** There are three signatures on this Libbey piece. **B.** This plate, cut fairly late, has a Hawkes signature. *Patrick Curry.* **C.** A nappy strongly resembling Hawkes's Gladys has an Egginton signature (marked, as usual, by a black dot). **D.** Although this plate is signed Tuthill, it looks more like Egginton. *Marie Hegarty.* **E.** A plate signed Hawkes that looks more like the work of Tuthill. *Rita Klyce.* **F.** Nappy signed Hoare does show his characteristic cluster cutting. *Patrick Curry*

Some very fine patterns cut early in the Brilliant Period have no signatures—we have never seen Hawkes's Chrysanthemum pattern signed, for example, and many beautiful pieces of glass cut at the height of the cut glass era have no signatures. On the other hand, signatures can designate quality, but we have also seen some very poor-quality pieces signed (Ill. 120).

Because of so much altering of patented designs, in 1895 both Hawkes and Libbey advertised that from that date forward they would sign all their glass. However, a unique bowl in our collection with a Hawkes signature exactly duplicates an unsigned one belonging to a friend. Out of twelve matching claret glasses in Strawberry-Diamond and Fan, only one bears the Hawkes signature. One Clark celery is signed, but its mate is not. Most people agree that the lowest paid and possibly the least responsible employee of a glass company stamped the signature. Understandably, pieces were carelessly skipped now and then (Ill. 121).

With Hawkes and Libbey taking the lead, other glass companies began to sign more of their glass. Thus, more signatures appear on pieces made after 1900.

120. On this 12-inch tray the Hawkes signature really designates a quality piece.

A

B

121A. An 11-inch celery signed Fry dates from his later period. *Sharalyn Spiteri.* **B.** This 9-inch celery tray with Clark signature comes from his best period of cutting. *George Clark.* **C.** The 11-inch celery signed Clark comes from his late period (dot marks the signature), but a matching tray is not signed.

C

Signature Confusions

Although a signature offers one positive means of identification, considerable confusion has developed relating to signatures. A good deal of this resulted from the fact that some companies changed signatures. Most glasshouses signed their glass with a trademark that they copyrighted; but after they had registered this, they would add to it or delete certain parts of it. Fry's trademark consisted of the name in script on a shield, but he signed his glass with only the script name (Ill. 122).

Between 1896 and 1919, Libbey used three signatures. A booklet from the Toledo Museum of Art lists the Libbey signatures as follows: Libbey with a sword under the name, 1896-1906; Libbey with the "L" and "Y" connected or unconnected, 1906-1913; Libbey with the "L" and "Y" connected but in a circle, 1919-1930. The booklet fails to mention a disconnected "L" and "Y" in a circle.

On a set of twelve sherry glasses signed Libbey, the company used two different signatures. The disconnected "L" and "Y" appear on the top of the foot on six glasses and under the foot on two; four are marked with the disconnected "L" and "Y" in a circle under the foot. Furthermore, the circleless signature is about a third the size of this same signature on a shot glass in our collection. Incidentally, we found the pattern of these sherry glasses listed as Jewel in a Libbey catalog dated 1904!

To add to the confusion, some companies used a specific signature for years before getting it copyrighted. J. Hoare & Company did not copyright the signature until May 12, 1900, although Hoare stated that he had used it since 1895. Hawkes registered his signature on March 3, 1903, but reported he had

122. Four signed vases, but with the signatures commonly used rather than the patented ones. **A.** A 14-inch vase signed Taylor Brothers between the rays of the star. *Helen Breeding.* **B.** An 8-inch vase with the script Fry under the foot, marked by a black dot. **C.** A 10-inch vase in Florence pattern signed by Hoare. *Roy Brown.* **D.** Another 11-inch vase with the J. Hoare signature. *Aubright Collection.* One Hoare vase has New York and the other has Corning on the signature.

A   B   C   D

94   used it since July, 1890. Egginton registered his signature January 23, 1906, seven years after he organized his company. A number of other companies—Tuthill, for one—never registered a signature.

Retailers and wholesalers sometimes used their own trademark on glass. A goblet signed by Averbeck also bears an Almy and Thomas signature (Ill. 89). Van Heusen, Charles & Company served as agents for Libbey and supposedly did no cutting; yet they signed glass (Ill. 109). The practice of adding the agent's name to the factory signature was apparently quite common in Canada.

Similarities in signatures also often cause confusion. Supposedly, Clark used a full maple leaf, but the Maple City Glass Company used a flat-base maple leaf. We have never seen any Clark signature but the script name; however, we have seen a number of pieces signed with a flat-base maple leaf (Ill. 124). In 1901, Libbey received a copyright for a signature consisting of a star in a circle, to place on pressed blanks. Some dealers and collectors confuse this trademark with the minute etched star in a circle, signature of Straus (Ill. 125).

By no means are all signatures large and highly visible. On occasion when we have pointed out a Sinclaire or Straus signature to someone, we usually hear the exclamation, "That tiny thing! It looks more like a scratch—except for its shape." These and the previously mentioned Libbey signatures fall into the minute category.

J. Hoare and Sons used two signatures. One included the date "1853"; the other, the word "Corning." Some people jump to the conclusion that 1853 is the date when the piece was cut. On the contrary, it is the date Hoare started his glass business in the United States. Bergen signed some pieces with two intersecting globes and others with the script name (Ill. 126).

In spite of all these confusing differences, collectors and dealers still rely on signatures for accurate identification, and search diligently for them.

123. Signatures vary from those on the patent records. **A.** This 10½-inch plate has the Libbey with saber signature. *George Clark.* **B.** A 12-inch plate designed by Walter A. Wood and patented January 31, 1899. It has the script Clark signature. **C.** The 8-inch plate here is a quality piece, signed Clark with the script signature. **D.** The 9-inch square orange bowl has the registered Hawkes signature. *Tisnado Collection*

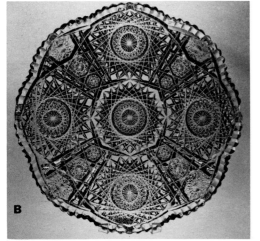

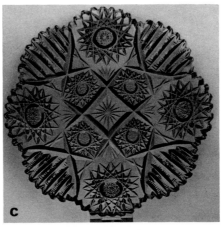

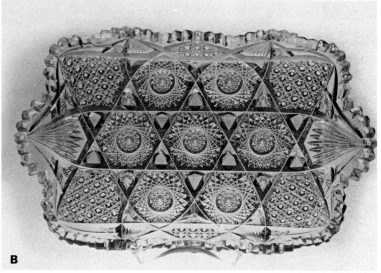

124A&B. Two signed Clark pieces with the script signature—a 9-inch square bowl and an oblong ice cream tray. *Hunt Collection*

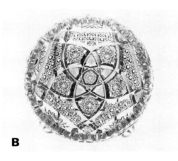
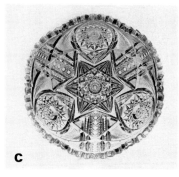
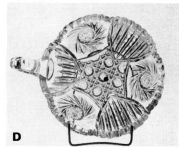

125. All these signed pieces do not appear characteristic of the glasshouse. **A.** A 6-inch nappy by Tuthill looks more like one that Taylor Brothers would cut. *Walker Collection.* **B.** This 9-inch bowl signed Straus resembles the Libbey style. *Hebel Collection.* **C.** A 9-inch bowl that does look like Pitkin & Brooks, as signed. *Hunt Collection.* **D.** The cutting on this 6-inch nappy appears similar to that on the one signed Clark, designed by Walter A. Wood (Ill. 123). Signature here is marked by the black dot.

126A. A 14-inch tray signed Hoare has New York on the signature. **B.** The cloverleaf tray is not signed. **C.** This 13-inch plate is Paola pattern by Dorflinger.

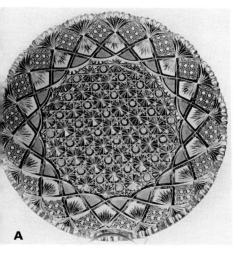

Locating Signatures

All companies etched their signatures. An employee pressed a rubber stamp with a trademark, monogram, or name on a pad saturated with a special acid formula. Then he pressed it firmly on a piece of glass, so that the acid adhering to the rubber stamp would etch the signature as a small milky imprint. Some signatures truly challenge discovery, either because of their inconspicuous location or small size, or because they are partly worn off (Ill. 127).

Dealers and collectors use various methods to locate signatures. One dealer claims that he finds them easily with a black light; another professes to find such equipment not only too expensive but not very helpful. A friend of ours has a black light topped by a magnifying glass, an arrangement that makes the signature fairly jump into view. However, this equipment is quite costly. A Fry signature can easily be located without equipment because it has a deep imprint. (Ill. 134)

A dealer of our acquaintance told us laughingly that when he put his wife's black nylon slip under a piece of signed glass, the signature stood out. Some prefer a fluorescent lamp or sunlight; others use an ordinary table lamp. We find sunlight excellent, especially late in the afternoon when the light appears even. One collector likes to use a flashlight with a plastic rim, he says, because the plastic gives off no reflections.

No matter what type of light is used or what method of detection is followed, the piece of glass must be rotated until the light reflects a mirrorlike surface. If the piece is then tipped or rocked slightly in various directions, or at an angle, the etched signature can be seen. Often, however, a faint Clark signature can be missed. (Ill. 127)

Even though a signature does not appear at once, do not give up completely. Later, it may unexpectedly pop into view. We inherited a celery tray but were never able to find a signature on it. Then, in lifting it from the cabinet one day, I suddenly saw the Clark signature. Now, whenever we fail to locate a signature, we say, "The signature is undiscovered."

Signature Placement

The etcher might place a signature in almost any blank spot on a piece, and so it pays to look everywhere. At times, the available space would not accommodate the entire signature—it may even be stamped over the cut pattern and thus have a gap in it. The employee entrusted with stamping the signature, if careless, might apply the stamp too lightly to produce a firm, clear signature; insufficient acid on the stamp would also result in a dim signature. On one bowl we saw, the signature had been stamped twice, giving a blurred effect. Wear will partially erase a signature, particularly one on the base or inside of a bowl. Between variation in placement, poor etching, and usage, finding some signatures is virtually a hunt for hidden treasure.

Some companies generally placed the signature in one particular spot; others varied its locations even on matching items. Of a dozen supremes signed Fry, half are signed on the inside center and the others under the foot near the rim. The signatures on bowls are usually easy to find. Here are both some common and some unique locations for signatures on various types of items:

A

B

C

127. The Clark signature on the base is most difficult to find. **A.** The cordial is signed on the base. **B.** Compote is also signed on the base. *Helen Breeding.* **C.** The 8-inch vase in Harvard by Libbey has a strong signature. *George Clark.* **D.** This nappy is by Mitchell, an unknown signature. *Walker Collection*

128. The Libbey signature is usually very strong, as it is on the covered cheese dish in **A.** *Rita Klyce.* **B.** This 6-inch-high flower center has a strong Hoare signature on the base. *Rita Klyce.* **C.** The Tuthill signature, often faint and in unusual places, is strong on the base of this footed banana bowl. *Hunt Collection.* **D.** A jardiniere, 7 inches high, has the signature of UGCO (Union Glass Company) on the liner, which is not shown. *Rita Klyce*

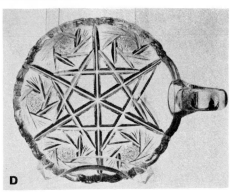

D

A

B

C

D

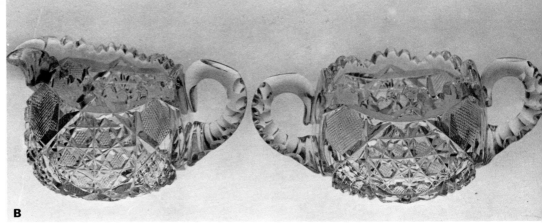

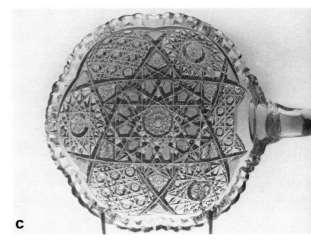

129. These three pieces have strong signatures. **A.** The 5-inch plate has the Tuthill signature—on the top center. **B.** This creamer and sugar signed Hoare have the signature on the inside center, but we have also seen the Hoare signature on the base of such items. **C.** The script Irving appears on the inside center with this pattern, which strongly resembles Libbey's Corinthian in general design. *Evelyn Henzi*

Bowls, Trays, Plates, Butter Pats, Relish Dishes

The inside center seems the favorite place for a signature on these items. Hoare usually signed a little off center, and the Libbey signature may be on the inside near the sawtooth rim. On a square Libbey bowl the signature is on an inside corner. We have also seen a Sinclaire and a Tuthill signature on the inside corner of oval trays. (See Ills. 130 and 145.)

Even with these pieces, however, signatures can be found in unique places. Both Libbey and Clark have signed along the face of a deep miter cut near the rim of a bowl. On one relish dish, the Hawkes signature appears in the split between the sides of a deep miter on the base.

Bottles, Carafes, Handleless Decanters, Flower Centers

Signatures on most of these pieces are on the base near the edge, on a clear place between the base and the side design, or between the neck and the side design. A carafe signed Libbey has the signature at the bottom of the flute on the neck. A dealer told us he had found a Fry signature on the rim of the mouth of a carafe, but a carafe signed Straus carries the signature an inch from the rim on the *inside* of the neck (Ills. 131 and 132).

Another dealer claims he has seen a Libbey signature under the extended rim of a wine decanter. Fry signed a flower center on a facet of the neck ring. A Hawkes medicine bottle is signed on the neck of the stopper.

Boxes: Powder, Patch, Jewel, Glove, Handkerchief

The most common places for a signature on a box, whether it is hinged or not, are the inside center of the base, the inside center of the lid, or the bottom, near the rim. Both lid and bottom will be signed when the box consists of two separate pieces. Hawkes signed the inside center of the lid and the inside center of the base on a powder box we own.

On boxes, most glass companies used the more ordinary locations for signatures rather than unique ones. Tuthill appears the exception. On a collar holder Tuthill signed on the rim edge of both the base and the lid (Ill. 133).

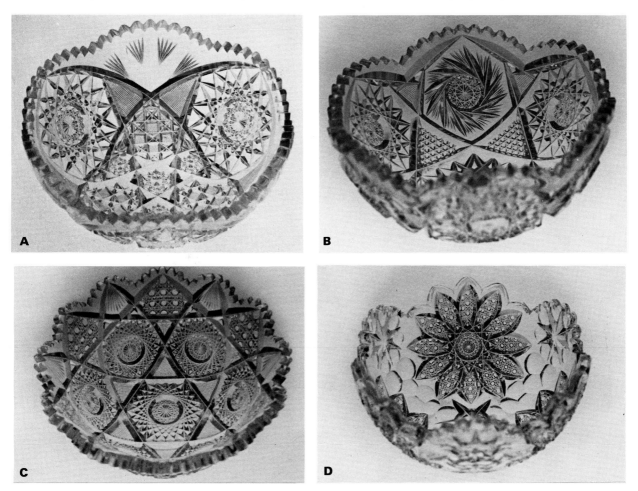

130. These 9-inch bowls have the signatures on the inside center. **A.** Tuthill signed this bowl a little off center. *Rita Klyce.* **B.** Irving signed this one in the center. *Roy Brown.* **C.** The Clark script signature on this piece is in the center. *Mildred Quinn.* **D.** The Hawkes signature is in the center. *Argie Burwell*

131A. Unsigned pitcher, 11 inches tall, has the simplicity of a Dorflinger pattern. **B.** Whiskey bottle has the Libbey signature on the neck flute. *George Clark*

132A. Water carafe has the Straus signature on the inside of the neck. *Roy Brown.* **B.** The Hawkes signature on the whiskey jug is at the end of the strap handle. *Walker Collection*

133. Tuthill signed both the top and the rim of the lid of this collar holder with "intaglio fruit."

134. Signatures appear on the flat of the handle of three of these pieces; one is signed on the base. **A.** Fry signed on the flat of the handle of this milk pitcher. **B.** The Libbey signature is on the flat of the handle of the water pitcher. *Roy Brown.* **C.** The Hoare signature is on the base of the cruet. **D.** Libbey signed on the flat of one handle of a three-handled loving cup. *Tisnado Collection*

Handled Pieces: Pitchers, Bowls, Cups, Spooners

Four basic locations were used for signatures on these pieces: the flat on the top of the handle, the inside center (of shallow items), underneath the handle, and the rim of the base. Hawkes generally signed on a clear spot directly under the handle. Clark signed more often on the rim of the base. (See Ill. 134.)

Dealers and collectors have reported various unusual places for signatures on handled items. One dealer reported finding a Tuthill and a Libbey signature under the lip. Pitkin and Brooks signed a sugar bowl on the side near the bottom on a clear diamond. Another dealer found a Libbey signature on the rim of the pitcher lip. Tuthill, Bergen, and Taylor Brothers sometimes signed between the rays of the star base (Ill. 122).

On a sugar and creamer, Wright signed on the flat of the handle and on the rim of the base, too (Ill. 111). Egginton signed a punch cup on the upper rim beside the handle. Fry signed a handled bowl on the inside where one handle joined the bowl. A lidded sugar bowl has the Tuthill signature on the lid rim that fits into the bowl part. Sometimes a sugar bowl and creamer are both signed in the same spot, sometimes not.

Pedestal Pieces: Compotes, Wines, Decanters, Cruets

Pedestal pieces may have the signature on the top edge of the foot, the under rim of the foot, or the inside center (if it is accessible). Clark generally signed on the rim of the base. Tuthill and Taylor Brothers usually signed between the rays of the star on the base. Hawkes and Libbey favored the top of the foot. However, we have an individual pedestal salt that Libbey signed on the base of the foot. One collector has found a Libbey signature on the stem of a compote, so there are always exceptions to the rule (Ill. 135).

Tubular Pieces: Tumblers, Spooners, Shot Glasses

The signature appears on the inside center or on the rim of the base on these items. Of two shot glasses signed by Libbey, one has the signature on the inside center and the other on the rim of the base; a spoon holder is signed on a clear spot near the sawtooth rim. The Libbey signature on a tumbler is on a clear square near the base (Ill. 89).

Other Shapes

The signature varies in location with the type of item. On a napkin ring it may be inside near the rim, on the rim itself, or on the outside in a clear spot. Baskets are usually signed on the inside center, the rim of the base, or under the handle (Ill. 136). Lamps generally have both the shade and the base signed in any clear spot near the rim.

A pair of candelabra has the Hawkes signature on the stem under the branches, but salt and pepper shakers are signed in the center of the base. On individual salts, Hoare signed the rim of the base and Hawkes the center of the base. Knife rests may show the signature on either a facet or the bar between the knobs. A collector has found a Fry signature on a facet of the glass handle of a ladle. Sinclaire signed a clock on the back near the top. Libbey's signature on candlesticks is on the top rim of the foot.

To sum up: A signature may be in a basic location or in a unique spot. Sometimes there seems to be none; but when you pick up the object or wash it, the signature jumps at you. Never give up without searching every clear spot and along each miter. Then look again.

135A. The flared Clark wines have the signature on the base. **B.** The supreme has the Hoare signature on the base. *Tisnado Collection*

136A. A 12-inch vase has the Libbey signature on a facet of the collar, near the base. *Helen Breeding.* **B.** The Tuthill signature is on the base of the basket. *Tisnado Collection.* **C.** This vase bears the Libbey signature near the top rim. *Aubright Collection*

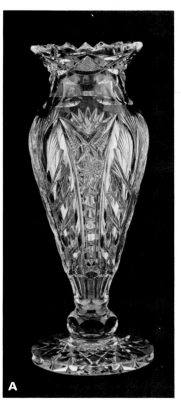
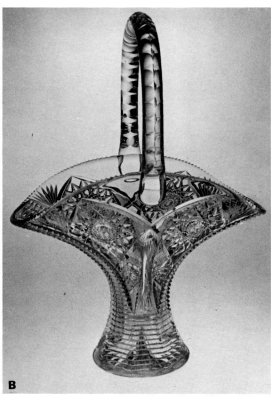
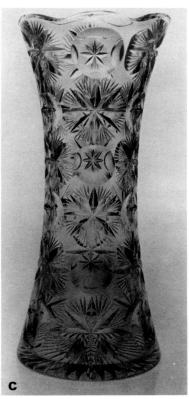

Unidentified Signatures

When we began researching signatures, we learned of a number of previously unpublished ones. Some of these we have identified and others we have not. From time to time collectors and dealers have written us about or showed us signatures in the hope that we could identify them. We have identified the following: Alford, Averbeck, Almy and Thomas, Lackawanna, Hobbs Gold Medal, Hunt Glass Company, Hope Glass Cutting Works, Majestic Glass Company, Sterling Glass Co., and Wright Glass Company.

Unfortunately, however, we have not been able to identify positively these signatures:

Script Arocke'

Recently a woman wrote us that she had found this signature etched on a water carafe; she thought it might once have contained an apostrophe and "s" that had worn off. Research has turned up absolutely no information.

Bonnet

A collector called our attention to this signature on the side of a punch cup. The word "Bonnet" is block printed across the cap part of an old-fashioned sunbonnet. We have found no clue to the identity of the signature.

C *Superimposed on* H

A collector has seen this signature, but our research has turned up nothing.

McD *in Block Print on Waving Banner*

A dealer showed us this signature on a relish dish. It was Phillip McDonald who designed the Russian pattern for Hawkes, and often master cutters eventually opened their own shops. We have not been able to verify that McDonald went into business for himself or to link this signature with him (Ill. 137).

Script Mitchell

A collector called our attention to this signature on a nappy. We have found nothing at all about a Mitchell.

Other Identifications

A number of companies used other means of identifying their products, some permanent, others not.

Labels

Christian Dorflinger & Sons of White Mills, Pennsylvania, and a number of other companies used a paper label on cut glass. William Iorio saw a piece of cut glass that contains the acid-etched signature of Dorflinger. The design is the same as that on the paper sticker. Understandably, most paper stickers have

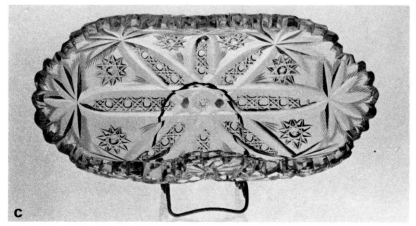

137. On these pieces, the signatures are located in the usual positions. **A.** This 7-inch spoon tray has the Hoare signature inside, slightly off center. *Patrick Curry.* **B.** The Clark signature is on the inside center of this 7-inch relish tray. *Hunt Collection.* **C.** McD Brothers, an unknown signature, appears in the inside center. *Rita Klyce.* **D.** The Hoare signature is a little off center on this piece.

long since been removed. In Albuquerque, New Mexico, we saw a dozen Dorflinger goblets with the original paper labels intact on every one. The dealer said he had bought them in what appeared to be the original packing case.

Silver Identification

When a company produced both the piece of glass and its silver lid or silver fittings, the identification generally was put on the silver part. Meriden Cut Glass Company (International Silver Company), Egginton, C. F. Monroe Company, and Pairpoint usually signed on the silver. On the other hand, we have seen Egginton and Sinclaire signatures sometimes on the silver and other times on the glass. (Ills. 138, 139) In our collection is a punch ladle with a cut glass handle marked "Dorflinger" in block letters on the silver stem, the only piece we have seen signed by this company. Although Hawkes made both the silver and the glass, the Hawkes signature generally is etched on the glass.

When one company did the cutting and another provided the silver parts, the silver carried the name of its manufacturer. Especially is this true of novelty pieces that the company probably bought from small unknown cutters. A silver lid on a small Vaseline jar bears the initials "I.S. Co." (International Silver Company). Another such jar has its silver lid marked "R.W. & S 1896," identified as R. Wallace & Sons Manufacturing Company. A third jar bears a banner "F & B" on it, the hallmark of Foster and Bailey, Providence, Rhode Island. Gorham Corporation and Rogers Brothers also marked silver appointments on cut glass.

138A&B. The Wilcox (Meriden) hallmark appears on top of a 9-inch bitters bottle and a 6-inch individual one. *Rita Klyce*

A   B

139. On all these items, silver is used to protect the crystal from chipping easily. **A.** This 9-inch plate with a silver rim bears a sterling mark only. **B.** A 7-inch pitcher has the Gorham hallmark. *Aubright Collection.* **C.** Candelabra signed Pairpoint has a crystal base for the silver holders. *C. W. Moody.* **D.** These 9-inch candlesticks with silver bases are signed Pairpoint. *C. W. Moody*

A whiskey bottle in our collection is marked with the name "Shreve & Company," a San Francisco jewelry store, on the silver stopper. The same company's trademark appears on the lid of an ink bottle. There are also ink bottles with silver lids marked "Tiffany & Company, Inc." (Ill. 140)

Liners

A number of cut glass items, such as champagne buckets, urns, ferneries, and spittoons, came with a nickel liner. A fernery in our collection has "U.G. Co. (Union Glass Company)—Somerville (Massachusetts)" on the liner. We have seen this same identification on a spittoon, champagne bucket, and jardiniere. Another fernery carries the name of "Shotten Cut Glass Company," Brooklyn, New York. It is logical to conclude that a company used this means of identification rather than an acid-etched signature. Of course loss of the liner means loss of the identification, and some liners carry no identification at all (Ill. 141).

140A. Inkwell marked Shreve on the sterling top. **B.** The two dresser jars bear the Wallace hallmark. **C.** The sterling top of this ink bottle is marked Tiffany.

141A. The liner for this footed vase bears no identification, but the pattern is identified in a Bergen catalog as Bedford. *Myra Mata.* **B.** The liner of the 7-inch-high spittoon carries the Union Cut Glass Company identification. *Rita Klyce.* **C.** The liner for the jardiniere also has the Union Cut Glass Company identification.

108 *Forgeries*

With the growing interest in identifying cut glass by signature, new discoveries will no doubt come to light. But this interest has also resulted in an increasing number of forged signatures. Some dealers have been approached by unscrupulous people who offered to forge signatures for them. The forger generally uses an electric needle. Such a signature can be felt with the fingernail; it is also easy to see. Etched signatures, on the other hand, cannot be felt and some can barely be seen.

There are more forgeries of names in script, such as Clark or Irving. One forger, instead of making a script "Irving," block-printed it on a relish dish. A forged Clark signature on a bowl almost succeeded—except for the fingernail test. At a recent antiques show, we saw a ten-inch plate in the Pitkin and Brooks Heart pattern that was signed Clark. We immediately suspected a forgery, and the fingernail test convinced us. We have also seen Hawkes printed in block letters and spelled "Hawks" on a basket obviously cut recently in Europe (Ill. 142). If the collector knows the original signature and has a good fingernail, forgers will not fool him.

Most dealers mark the location of the signature on a piece of cut glass if they find it, but sometimes the collector who knows patterns or even the identifying motifs finds a signature the dealer has missed.

142. A basket in modern cut, representative of the lead crystal coming in from Europe, has the word "Hawks" put on with an electric needle near the top of the handle. The forger needs to do some research into spellings.

6.

THE

BUYING GAME

MOTIVATION FOR BUYING CUT GLASS VARIES WITH THE COLLECTOR AND the dealer. Some collectors find the exquisite beauty and rarity of cut glass inspiration enough to begin a collection. Others feel much the same, but they also consider cut glass a good investment. A few collectors view cut glass purely as a safe investment that will appreciate in value. Primarily, the dealer buys for regular customers or to develop new ones, but always to make a profit.

Most collectors and dealers have made mistakes in buying because of lack of knowledge or failure to spot defects that reduce the value of a piece of cut glass. Such mistakes can happen to anyone who buys regularly—we have made our share of them too. Finally, we asked a number of collectors and dealers how they avoided such errors. They told us what to look for and explained how to make a very careful inspection of any item. They also pointed out that although some defects completely spoil a piece, others only reduce its value.

Damaged Pieces

Most dealers list brilliant cut glass either as "mint" or "as is." No doubt they borrowed the term "mint" from coin collectors, to indicate perfect condition or only the most minor defects. "As is" indicates some very obvious damage. Since old American cut glass came off the production line some seventy-five to a hundred years ago, few pieces remain undamaged today. Occasionally, pieces that have been stored and never used are still in perfect condition, but these are the exception. Therefore, it is a good idea to follow the example of serious collectors and careful dealers and carry along a pocket magnifying glass that will make it easier to detect difficult-to-see defects.

110 *Chips*

A chip may be either a small nick or a sizable hunk broken off a piece of cut glass. Age as well as heavy cutting can cause this type of glass to chip more easily than other types. Chips appear principally along edges, either on the top or bottom. For example, a chip is often found somewhere along the top edge of a piece—on the lip of a pitcher or decanter or the sawtooth rim of a bowl or compote. Sometimes an entire tooth has been knocked off a serrated edge. Slight nicks are likely to be found on a deep-cut facet or miter that has bumped against the wall of a cabinet or against another piece. Examine the edge of footed pieces and the bases of tumblers—in fact, look everywhere for chips (Ill. 143).

Most chips can be easily located by running the fingers along the edges and the miters. With practice, the collector will learn to feel the slightest irregularity. For chips on miter cuts or the star motif, however, trace each part of the design with the forefinger or examine it with a magnifying glass. In the case of pieces like bowls or compotes, look through them from the inside—chips can generally be spotted from this angle, and a magnifying glass will verify their location.

Flakes

A flake differs slightly from a chip. It is a thinner layer that splits from the glass—most often near a rim—and generally does not feel so sharp to the touch as a chip. Running a finger around the rim of a tumbler may not even detect a flake, but if you grasp the edge between forefinger and thumb and move slowly around the rim, you will feel the flake (Ill. 144).

On a bowl-shaped item, the flake may occur on the inside or the outside, starting at the sawtooth edge. Pedestal pieces flake on the stem or foot. On pitchers, flakes occur under the lip or near the handle; on decanters and carafes, near the top rim. The rims of glasses and tumblers flake easily.

143A. A tobacco jar, like this one signed Hoare, may chip around the rim unless great care is taken in replacing the lid. *George Clark.* **B.** A chip on this finger bowl might easily be ground out because there is a wide clear band at the top.

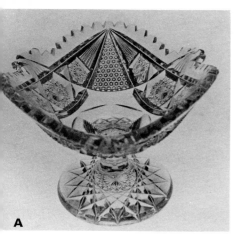

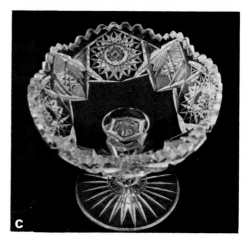

144. Pedestal pieces are likely to flake on the foot and pitchers on the rim. If either of these compotes (**A** & **C**) was used often for flowers with a frog, it might well become scratched. *Patrick Curry.* **B.** A flake sliced off the rim of this pitcher could not be repaired because of the high placement of the handle. *George Clark*

Bruises

The term "bruises" is used to refer to the multitude of tiny scratches that produce a cloudiness on the base of a piece or the inside of a bowl or compote. Many collectors and dealers call these age or wear marks. Since they indicate age, counterfeiters have put them on new pieces to pass them off as old. Any good lead crystal shows a strong sensitivity to scratching.

Look for bruises mostly on the bases of pieces, where they may have rubbed against rough surfaces, particularly on bowls, vases, pitchers, and the like. Flower frogs (holders) will leave bruise marks on any piece used to hold flowers. Some of the larger companies learned to use crosshatching or similar motifs on the spots where a piece would come into contact with a surface; this practice prevented or disguised bruise marks. The bases of tumblers, stemware, or compotes are the most likely to show bruises because of frequent rubbing against the surface of a table or shelf (Ills. 145 and 146).

A magnifying glass clearly shows up the depth of such scratches. When the scratches are not too deep, a professional glass company can buff them off and restore the mirror finish, but if the scratches do not mar the beauty of the piece, let them remain as evidence of authenticity.

Fractures

A fracture—a myriad of tiny cracks—results from accidentally hitting two pieces of glass together or against some hard surface. You may not be able to feel these small cracks, but you can easily see them—and they mar the beauty of a piece of glass. Look for fractures on the rims of tumblers and stemware, the necks of carafes and wine decanters, and the top rims of bowls and compotes. Examine any piece that might have come into regular contact with another, such as a pitcher and tumbler set or covered cheese and butter dishes. Other pieces too can develop fractures.

Avoid buying a piece with a fracture because the damaged part may crack off no matter how carefully the piece is handled. Also, you can do nothing whatsoever to remove or correct a fracture.

Cracks

A crack is an actual cleavage in the glass, whether or not it can be felt. Because of the age of cut glass, its lead content, and the deep cutting, it cracks

145A. This square bowl in Corinthian pattern, signed Libbey, was so badly scratched that it looked sick. The scratches were buffed out. **B.** The 12-inch plate might easily suffer bruising because there is a clear ring around the hobstar center. *Tisnado Collection*

146A. A 10-inch double-handled bowl in a Harvard variant, like this one, would never show bruises. *Patrick Curry.* **B.** This 9-inch berry bowl in another Harvard variant is protected from bruises by its crosshatched buttons.

147. Pieces with deep and intricate cutting have a greater tendency to crack. This beautiful shallow 11-inch bowl is in mint condition.

easily—especially when exposed to extreme temperatures, either too hot or too cold. A piece in our collection cracked while merely sitting in the cabinet.

Sometimes cracks will follow a deep miter, and when they do, they are almost impossible to locate (Ill. 147). Drinking glasses crack along the top edge; applied handles may crack and break off at the point where applied. Decanters crack around the neck where the stopper fits—simply trying to remove a stopper or pushing it too tightly into the neck may crack the decanter.

To locate a crack, hold the piece to the light and carefully examine it from the inside, if possible. If this is not feasible, use strong light and a magnifying glass. A crack on an uncut surface usually shows up clearly, but one on a heavily cut surface may prove a challenge. If a piece has a large chip or flake, begin at that point and check carefully to see if a crack resulted.

Some glasshouses—Hawkes and Dorflinger, for example—added silver rims as decoration. Carefully check such pieces to be sure a silver rim was not added later specifically to hide chips or cracks. A highly decorated rim is likely to have been on a piece from the beginning. Cracks often develop when silver fittings are removed if they are not taken off correctly. Examine with particular care boxes and other items where the silver has been replated. Replated silver looks too shiny and new. On some replated pieces, however, the silver has been oxidized to make it more nearly resemble the original finish. Some collectors and dealers insist that any replating restores the original value, but others disagree, and so dealers often will not tell you that a piece has had a silver job. In spite of the excellent replating and oxidation on the silver fittings of a syrup pitcher signed Hawkes, we challenged the dealer. He denied the replating until we pointed out that the person who replaced the silver fittings put the signature on the side rather than in the usual place under the handle (Ill. 148).

148. A silver band may hide a chip, flake, or crack. **A.** This syrup pitcher is signed Hawkes on the side rather than under the handle, indicating that a replating job was done. **B.** The fact that the silver band on this heavily cut compote is a decorated one indicates that the band was on the compote originally. *Roy Brown.* **C.** A silver top protects this champagne pitcher from chipping; it was part of the original design. *Marie Hegarty*

A   B   C

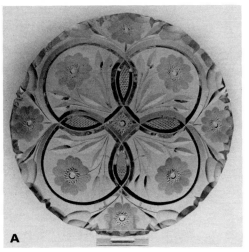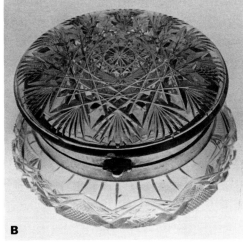

149A. A cutter removed four flakes on the rim of this 7-inch plate by cutting intaglio flowers there. **B.** Silver fittings hide the crack in the rim of the top on this hinged box, signed Hoare.

A crack may run so close to a silver rim that it goes unnoticed. At a flea market, before we bought a small jewel box with a silver rim, we examined it for damage and saw none. Later at home, when I washed it, there was a strong smell of glue. A little soaking in warm water dissolved the glue so that the rim came off—and then it became obvious to us that someone had once pried off the silver and broken the glass. The silver rim had completely hidden this damage and repair (Ill. 149). Another time, a dealer suggested that we buy a heavily cut tobacco jar with a badly chipped rim and have a silver band added to conceal the damage—a suggestion we did not take. Now we always examine pieces with silver bands with special care. If a plain silver rim appears on a piece where one would not ordinarily expect to find such a rim or in places that chip easily, the experienced collector gets suspicious. In conclusion: Never knowingly buy a cracked piece of glass.

Heat Checks

When the gaffer applied the handle to an item, he tried to keep the temperature of the piece and the handle exactly the same. If he failed to maintain the correct temperature for both, or if the handle cooled too quickly, a tiny white line, or *heat check,* would appear where he attached the handle. Most heat checks occur at the upper end of a handle. (Since the gaffer applied the lower end of the handle first, the upper end had more time to cool.) In our experience we have noticed heat checks more often on pieces cut by Libbey than by other companies.

Some collectors and dealers believe a handle will break at the point of a heat check. We have seen some handles broken along this line, but we have also seen others that have not broken. Certainly a heat check weakens a handle, so take precautions with such a piece. Most dealers and collectors readily admit that a heat check reduces the value of a piece.

Sometimes handles do not adhere completely to the body of the item—in fact, you may be able to put the tip of a fingernail between the handle and the body of the article. We bought a basket with a handle like this. Although no heat check showed, the basket handle cracked where it did not adhere to the body.

Before you buy any article with a handle, look inside at the spot where the handle joins the body. The glass here should appear clear. If you see a tiny white line at this point, call it to the dealer's attention and ask for a better price. In short, make sure the handle fits snugly against the body of the piece.

Sick Glass

Most dealers and collectors quickly recognize one type of "sick glass"—it has a slightly cloudy or frosted appearance inside, particularly in decanters, cruets, and salt shakers. The acidity of vinegar, wine, salt, or perfume causes a chemical reaction that oxidizes the inner surface. Some authorities, on the other hand, blame this oxidation on a too-high alkaline content in the glass batch.

If you put water or liquid in a sick piece of glass, the white disappears and does not reappear until the glass dries. Oil, Glass Wax, or a nonstick cooking spray will make a sick piece look as if someone had washed the item and not dried it. Avoid buying any piece with this beaded wetness. A small amount of rubbing alcohol will dry a wet decanter immediately and reveal the sick appearance. Some people will claim they have not washed the item, but remember—if the owner could have washed out the cloudiness, he would have done so, to get a better price. Never believe anyone who claims the "sickness" will wash out of a piece of glass.

Another type of glass sickness consists of a residue that forms in the bottom of decanters, bottles, or vases that have not been properly cleaned. Sometimes these deposits will come out if the glass is soaked.

In a third type of sick glass, the crystals separate as a result of imperfect fusion of the metal. When the glass item is held against a strong light, a web of minute fissures can be seen. Some authorities say that such glass will eventually shatter. As previously mentioned, Mr. Gerould called this scissile glass, and suggested that cooling too quickly might have caused the defect. In his opinion, such an item would not explode. There is absolutely nothing to be done about scissile glass.

All types of sickness may develop in a piece of glass, or perhaps only one. As for buying such glass, never do so—unless you want to experiment with a piece that has the sediment type of sickness.

Descriptions and Misconceptions

Experience offers the best route to more astute buying. The careful collector soon learns to recognize clever deceptions and innocent misconceptions. Here are some of the more common ones.

Repaired Pieces

Whether a repaired piece should bring full price or not is a matter of debate in antiques circles. Some argue that skilled repairs restore the beauty of a piece. Others contend that a repaired piece is no longer wholly original, and that—in some categories of collecting—repairs have been known to alter the intent or purpose of a piece. The truth of the matter is that much depends on the repairs themselves. In the case of cut glass, expert cutters do an excellent job of restoration that could fool a connoisseur; less skilled ones can botch a repair job. Be that as it may, some collectors will not buy a damaged piece; others will—and then proceed to have it repaired. Certain dealers always have a damaged item repaired because their customers insist on mint-condition pieces. A good many dealers prefer to sell "as is" and let the customer himself decide whether restoration is advisable.

Stemware is frequently chipped, so always look for repairs. Originally, stemmed pieces had a slight bulge right below the rim, the result of fire polishing at the factory. A grinding job removes a part or all of this bulge. Originally, also, the edges curved. If the stemware has been ground down, a poor job will leave the edges flat and sharp to the touch, but a good job rounds off the edges. Run the fingers along the top rim to test for sharpness. Also set the glass upside down on a flat surface and see if it rocks, indicating an unevenness or warp caused by a poor grinding job. In a set of glasses, make sure all are the same height. Too much variation in height indicates some have been ground (Ill. 150).

Pieces with sawtooth rims have a high rate of casualty. In checking the rims of these, note whether one point is cut down farther than another, as it might be if a repair had been made of a broken or chipped point. On both sawtooth pieces and stemware, also note whether the edge comes too close to the design or cuts into the pattern (Ill. 150). Originally such pieces had a clear band at the top.

Some expert repairmen can remove broken handles and fill in the space with cutting. Make sure that all the design motifs match exactly. If one seems a bit different, perhaps it was added to conceal the absence of a handle that should have been in that spot. We have seen cups, nappies, and sugar bowls (to mention a few) on which the handles have been removed and a similar design cut on the blank surface.

Check the lip on a pitcher. Is it too stubby for the body, or does the spout turn downward too much? The rim of a water carafe normally is of equal thickness all around. If one part appears considerably thinner than the other, perhaps a flake was ground off (Ill. 151). The foot of a pedestal piece chips easily in spite of its rounded rim. If the rim is not rounded or the points of the star on the bottom come too close to the edge, someone has probably had a grinding job done on the piece. The same is true when the foot looks too small for the top. In extreme cases, a skilled cutter may even create a new design or recut the old one after removing chips, and such repairs sometimes prove almost impossible to detect.

Adapted Pieces

When an item is so chipped that not even an expert can see any way to restore it, a good cutter may adapt it—that is, alter it into a quite different piece. Always examine a rare-looking piece carefully. We have seen a bulbous water carafe converted into a rose bowl by removing the neck; another carafe had its neck cut down and a stopper fitted into it. Careful inspection of, say, a toothpick holder may show that it was made by cutting off the broken top of a salt or pepper shaker; chipped juice glasses have been ground down to whiskey tumblers. When broken handles are removed from a sugar bowl or punch cup, these pieces can easily be mistaken for rare handleless items. A foot broken from a pedestal piece can be converted into a paperweight; a compote with a broken pedestal may become a nappy, and a broken-handled nappy can turn into a large ice cream or berry dish. The bottom of a broken tubular vase may be listed as a coaster for a wine bottle. When an article appears exceptionally rare, the experienced collector stands back and takes a long second look.

150. Two poor repair jobs where cutting on the rims went into the pattern. **A.** Champagne glass in Radiant pattern by Mt. Washington. **B.** Rosebowl in Wheat by Hoare.

151A. One side of the rim on this water carafe is thinner than the other, indicating a repair job. **B.** When the lip of this pitcher cracked off, the craftsman glued it back, then cut a miter over the crack and a matching miter underneath the lip on the other side.

118   *Mismated Pieces*

To the average person, a hobstar creamer seems to match almost any hobstar sugar. However, the minor motif on the sides should match too. Possibly more mismatched sugar and creamers are sold than any other mismatched pairs.

When buying a pitcher with tumblers, make sure that the tumblers match both the major and the minor motif of the pitcher. We have seen a pitcher with hobstars sold with buzzstar tumblers as a matched set. Make sure that all the tumblers match, too. Wineglasses should match the decanter; shot glasses or whiskey tumblers should match the jug (Ill. 152).

Plates are other items that have a high casualty rate. When buying a mayonnaise bowl, always make sure that the underplate is a genuine match. In the case of a butter or cheese dish, the dome and the bottom must form a perfect marriage. A plate must also have the same design as the butter or ice tub it ac-

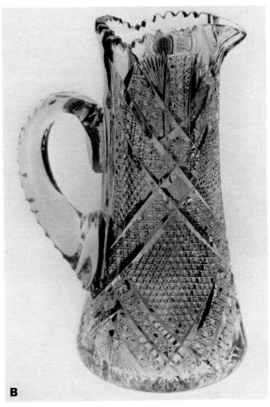

152. Pairs must match. **A.** This tumbler matches the pitcher in **B.** *Barbara W. Doble.* **C.** Tumble-up glass matches the carafe with strawberry-diamond motif. *Rita Klyce.* **D.** Matching salad bowl and plate in Russian by Pairpoint. *George Clark*

companies. Other articles sometimes mismated are the shade and base of a lamp, the two parts of a punch bowl (base and bowl), an ice cream platter and its plates, and a berry bowl and the individual berry dishes (Ill. 153).

Stoppers frequently get broken or lost, and so make sure to look for the number on the base or cylinder of the stopper and the matching one on or near the neck of the article. When a stopper is cut with a matching design, it is easy to tell that it belongs with the item. A perfume lapidary stopper has a very short neck, and a cruet or decanter lapidary stopper has a slender one. Sometimes perfume stoppers have been substituted in cruets and cruet stoppers in perfume bottles. As a final test, see if the stopper rocks in the bottle. If it does, the two do not belong together. Remember that a ground stopper is meant to fit into a ground neck. Beware of an item with a ground stopper and a neck that is not ground. Your best safeguard is knowing through study and experience what type of stopper a piece should have (Ills. 154-156).

153. Here are other matching pairs. **A.** Mayonnaise bowl and plate. *Patrick Curry.* **B.** The bowl matches the plate, a variant of Colombia pattern by Blackmer Cut Glass Company. *Marie Hegarty.* **C.** The 10-inch plate matches the dome of the butter dish. *George Clark.* **D.** The dish for the pound block of butter matches the individual butter pat. *George Clark*

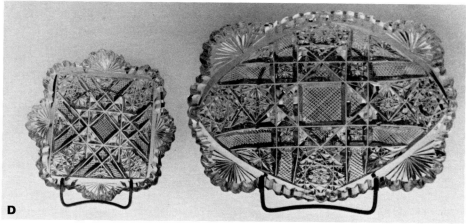

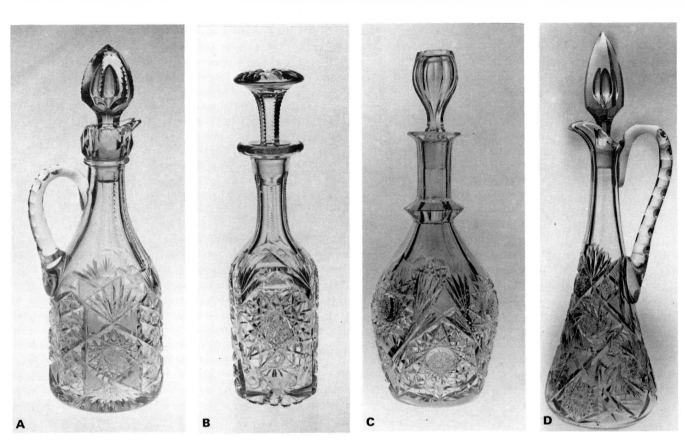

154. These stoppers and bottles match. **A.** The wine decanter has a numbered teardrop stopper. *Walker Collection.* **B.** This is a typical stopper for a Worcestershire bottle, the hobstar on top repeating that on the side. *George Clark.* **C.** The stopper with the teardrop in this wine decanter repeats the shape of the bottle. *George Clark.* **D.** The ground stopper and the ground neck go together on this sherry decanter. *Patrick Curry*

155. The cruet stopper in **A** is the right one, but the cruet stopper in Hoare's Monarch pattern perfume bottle (**B**) is wrong. **C.** The stopper in the cruet is pressed glass, and the one in the bottle does not match the pattern and is the wrong shape. The bottle is Devonshire pattern by Hawkes.

156A. The wine decanter by Hawkes has a cologne stopper rather than the correct one. **B.** The signed Clark decanter also obviously has the wrong stopper. **C.** This handled wine decanter has the correct stopper.

Wrong Identification

Some people lump small dishes into the general categories of relishes, nappies, and bonbons. But many of the major companies produced a variety of small pieces in shapes and sizes that experienced dealers and collectors have now learned to identify otherwise from old catalogs. On the other hand, some companies cut pieces for table use that served multiple purposes. A catalog from an unidentified company advertised a "Fancy Dish for spoons, bonbons, jelly, olives, pickles, etc." The dimensions were 7 ¾ inches by 4 ¾ inches; this dish was only 1 ½ inches in depth. Even major companies did not differentiate greatly between the nappy and the bonbon dish. Consequently no one can set specific rules for the identification of pieces, but here are some useful general characteristics.

Because of the popularity of miniatures, a few dealers and collectors tend to lump all small pieces in that category. A Victorian place setting included many small items, and these might vary in size. An individual nut dish can range in length from 2 ½ to 4 ½ inches and in width from 1 ½ to 2 ½ inches. In shape, it may be round, oval, square, or triangular. The individual olive dish or tray, often incorrectly called a miniature celery because of its shape, measured 3 ½ by 2 ½ inches or 4 ½ by 3 inches.

Individual salts sometimes came in sets with a master salt, which might have a pedestal and be of a different shape from the individual ones. The diameter of individual salts varied from 1 inch (the size sometimes wrongly labeled a miniature) to 2 ½ inches. A salt measuring 3 ½ to 4 inches would be considered a master salt. Most of the salts were round, but there are also oval, square, and triangular ones.

The Victorian place setting also included individual butter pats, sometimes called butter chips. The catalogs give the dimensions of these as 2 inches. A butter plate or "butterette" measured 3 ½ inches. Some people confuse the butter plate with the coaster, as the two have the same measurement. The coaster, however, has a definite raised rim; the butter plate has a flattened edge like a dinner plate.

The knife rest was made in numerous sizes and lengths. The smaller ones are individual knife rests; the larger are for the master carving knife. Another item of a table setting, the napkin ring, could be from an inch to 4 inches wide.

Some dealers and collectors mistake individual berry bowls for nappies. These small bowls matched a large one and measured 4 ½ to 5 inches in diameter and 1 ½ to 2 inches in depth. Generally speaking, a nappy has the same depth but measures 5 to 7 inches. The wider dimension gives the nappy a shallower look. You can easily recognize the common one-handle nappy and the rarer two- and three-handle ones.

Frequently a bonbon dish was made with a heavier blank than the nappy and had a rarer shape. Although some were round like the nappy, most were shaped like a square, heart, diamond, squat oval, or triangle. On some bonbon dishes one side is expanded for use as a handle or grip. A bonbon dish can be 7 or 8 inches in length or diameter.

The olive or pickle tray, the spooner, and the relish are all sometimes confused with the bonbon dish by today's collectors. The relish dish usually measures 7 to 8 inches in length and about 3 inches in width. The olive or pickle tray is about the same length as the relish, but an inch or two wider. The spooner or spoon tray resembles the olive or pickle dish, but its ends are usually flattened so that the spoons lie easily in the cradle. On bonbon, pickle or olive, and relish dishes the ends are raised.

Another area of confusion pertains to bread and celery trays. The celery tray varies in length from 11 to 14 inches and in width from 4 ½ to 5 ½ inches. The bread or roll tray may be the same length but is at least two inches wider. Both have the same shape—oval or rectangular.

Ice cream trays also come in rectangular or oval shape, but they were made from extremely heavy blanks measuring 12 to 14 inches in length and as much as 8 inches in width. The shape of some such oval trays narrows almost to a rounded point at either end, and dealers sometimes refer to this kind of tray as an "ice cream platter." We have not found an ice cream tray described as a platter in any of the catalogs we studied. An ice cream set consisted of a tray and matching plates or saucers 6 inches in diameter. Some sets did include handled nappies.

Ice cream plates, along with the plate that came with a mayonnaise bowl, ice tub, and covered butter or cheese dish, are frequently sold as individual plates and not as parts of broken sets. The plate belonging to a covered butter dish measures 5 to 7 inches, and to a covered cheese dish, 8 to 10 inches, depending on the company that produced it. Except for the difference in size, the two look exactly alike. You can feel a slight circular indentation on plates that once held bowls or domes. The ice cream plate will not have this round depressed area in the center.

A study of old catalogs not only will familiarize the collector and dealer with the shapes and sizes of items cut by American companies, but also help him to identify the pieces correctly. More important, such knowledge provides a sound basis for confidence in buying.

Foreign Glass

American cut glass so surpassed English, Irish, and Bohemian glass that the difference is not hard to recognize. These glasses lack the heavy weight, clarity, and detailed pattern that make American cut glass superior. According to the Higgins & Seiter catalog, an American ambassador to Russia bet a Russian host that the United States made the finest cut glass in the world. When Higgins & Seiter sent the merchandise, the Russian nobleman paid off the bet without argument.

Canadian Glass

For several reasons, Canadian cut glass is sometimes easy to confuse with glass made in the United States. Many Canadian companies bought blanks from American glassmakers, such as Corning or Libbey, and a number of American cutters at one time worked for Canadian companies, as the Egginton brothers did for the St. Lawrence Glass Company. Furthermore, agents in Canada sold American cut glass but under different signatures. Finally, several Canadian companies cut motifs similar to those used by American factories.

On the other hand, it is easy to recognize pieces cut on blanks made in Canada or bought from European companies. The glass of these blanks was made from a lime rather than lead formula and has a grayish tint.

Gowans, Kent & Company, Limited, Toronto

H. G. Clapperton organized this company in 1900. It cut such exclusive patterns as Butterfly, Wheat, and Maple Leaf as well as geometric designs. Cassidy Limited later took over the company (Ill. 157).

Gundy-Clapperton Company, Toronto

We have found more signed glass from this company founded by G. H. Clapperton in 1905. Later Mr. Clapperton founded the Quinte-Clapperton Amalgamated in Deseronto, Ontario. Fire destroyed that plant in 1931. The company did not manufacture glass but purchased blanks from La Compagnie des Cristalleries de Baccarat in France, the Val St. Lambert glassworks in Belgium, and Libbey Glass Company. They developed a reputation for good floral and geometric designs cut by fine craftsmen. Pattern names included Mayflower, Colonies, Maple Leaf, Metro, and Coronation. The company signed many of their pieces, and also often added the name of the agent to their own acid-etched signature. Hence, the Gundy-Clapperton cloverleaf is also found combined with the names of such agents as Birks, Dingwall, or G. B. Allen (see Appendix). (Ills. 158 and 159.)

Wallaceburg Cut Glass Company, Wallaceburg, Ontario

J. F. Singleton was hired as the manager of this firm at one time; it specialized in lightly cut floral patterns. We have seen no evidence that the glass was signed. In operation from 1913 to 1930, the company made a fairly complete line of cut glass: baskets, bonbon dishes, stemware, cake plates, water sets, and candlesticks, to name a few items. Some of these were in rose-colored glass.

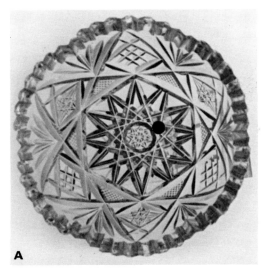

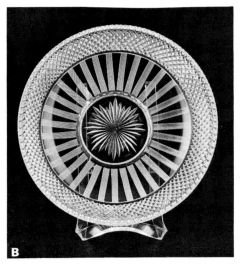

157. Three pieces of signed Canadian glass. **A.** A 5-inch berry dish signed by Gowans, Kent & Company (at the black dot). **B.** An 8-inch shallow bowl signed with an unidentified signature: NACGMO. *C. W. Moody.* **C.** Vase, 17½ inches high, signed Watson Brothers, Calgary, Alberta, Canada.

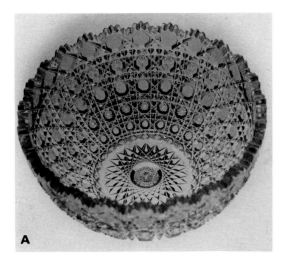

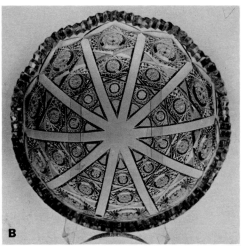

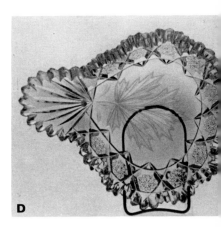

158. More glass of the Gundy-Clapperton Company than of other Canadian companies is available in the United States. **A.** This 9-inch bowl is signed by CGCo and Birks. *Elizabeth Hazlett.* **B.** An 8-inch bowl with the CGCo only, in a design similar to Hawkes's Panel pattern. **C.** An 8-inch berry bowl signed CGCo and Dingwall. *Hunt Collection.* **D.** Candy nappy with the single signature C. G. Co. *Rita Klyce*

159A. This pitcher in a pattern similar to Hawkes's Queens is signed CGCo. **B.** Wine decanter signed CGCo on the base. *George Clark*

House of Birks, Montreal

This company became better known for silver products, but it operated a glass factory in Montreal. By 1894, it employed eleven glass cutters. George Phillips & Company bought the factory in 1907, but Birks continued as an agent for the glass factory. We have also seen the Birks signature on glass produced by Gundy-Clapperton Company and Roden Brothers.

Roden Brothers, Toronto

More and more glass appears in shops and shows these days with the signature of Roden Brothers; they used the letter R flanked by lions. We have seen this signature on a sugar and creamer, bedside tray, and nappy, all cut in floral designs (Ill. 160). Like Gundy-Clapperton Company, Roden Brothers added the name of the agent to their own signature. We have found pieces with acid-etched signatures of both Roden and Birks or of Roden and Porte & Markle.

Other Canadian cut glass companies were the Ottawa Cut Glass Company, Belleville Cut Glass Company, Watson Brothers, and Lakefield Cut Glass Company. Lakefield featured the Lakefield pattern (Ill. 161). Two dealers have told us they believe the signature NACGMO is also that of a Canadian company. According to some reports, glass is still being cut in Canada today. A cutter who does repair work on cut glass told us he had been offered a job with a Canadian company as a cutter, but he was reluctant to name the

160A. A 9-inch-high compote signed in the center of the bowl by Roden Brothers.
B. The cream pitcher has the same signature. *Mrs. A. L. Moreggia*

161. A 12-inch-high compote identified as the Lakefield pattern, of the Lakefield Cut Glass Company of Canada.

162A. Two glasses cut recently in Canada. **B.** The plate is also modern.
C. A 12-inch vase in modern cut.

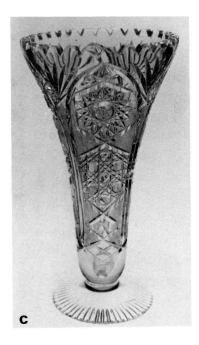

company. Also, a collector showed us cut glass tumblers recently bought from a Canadian factory; they were of very thin glass and had thick bases. Unfortunately, she was unable to recall the name of the factory (Ill. 162).

Modern Cut Glass

Today gift shops and department stores sell modern lead crystal cut in Germany, Portugal, Italy, Scotland, Austria, Belgium, France, and Ireland. According to law, a label must designate the country of origin, but of course labels are easily removed. Some of this glass is quite heavy and has overall cutting. We have seen pieces of it in antiques shows offered as old American cut glass or old Irish Waterford. The better-cut modern pieces have actually fooled experienced dealers, but—with study—you can learn to recognize modern cut glass (Ill. 163).

For one thing, modern cut glass is made in shapes Americans never cut. Covered candy dishes and vases may have odd little curved legs. American-made ferneries and a few odd pieces did have legs, but these were straight and loglike. Modern decanters are cone shaped, with wide-spreading bases. Pitchers have long slender necks, and the stoppers in decanters may be pressed glass. Most sugar bowls have lids, but lidded sugar bowls are rare in American cut glass. Some compotes have bases an inch thick. Modern cut glass baskets do not have applied handles—the entire piece is cut from a single block of glass.

Cutting costs are high today, and so modern factories favor large clear diamonds, fans, thumbprints, or buzzes rather than more complicated motifs. Flowers cut on pressed blanks decorate many pieces. A few of the more expensive pieces have hobstars, but otherwise the flat or elongated star is more common. A chain of crosshatched diamonds or clusters of clear cane give an illusion of heavy cutting.

The cutting on modern glass generally is smooth and greasy to the touch; this indicates the glass has been acid polished or a figured blank has been used. Crosshatching and stars have a whitish cast and, lacking a good polish, consequently feel rough to the touch.

Although modern cut glass will ring, it does not have the deep bell tone of

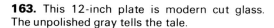

163. This 12-inch plate is modern cut glass. The unpolished gray tells the tale.

164. A pedestal bowl in modern cut.

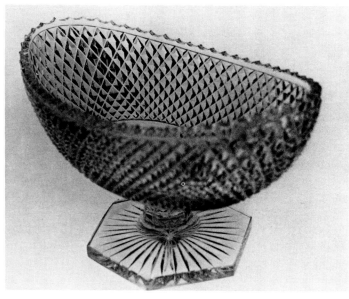

old cut glass. It feels heavy, but much of its weight is concentrated in the base of the piece. Even though modern glass is clear, it lacks the luster of old cut glass. Keep all these points in mind, and you will not mistake pieces of modern European for old American cut glass (Ill. 164).

Colored Cut Glass

A good deal of colored cut glass has come into this country recently from France, Germany, Austria, and other European countries, and much of it has found its way into the antique market as old American colored cut glass. Here are some guidelines for distinguishing between the modern and the old: Most of the new glass has only the thin layer of color that is characteristic of flashing—this bleeds into the clear. American cut glass shows a sharp line of division because the color was an overlay of glass rather than flashing. In addition, American colored-cut-to-clear shows a deeper tone. Much of the imported glass is in a pale cranberry or green.

Imported colored glass has the same American motifs—the buzz and hobstar, for example—but it lacks the detail and precision of cutting of old glass. Also, more thumbprints and flutes are used. Beware especially of rare shapes. Much of the new colored glass consists of wine sets and stemware. Any time you see a dozen matching stemmed pieces, think twice before you buy.

In the final analysis, the buying game must rest on a solid foundation of knowledge and experience. Examine carefully any piece of cut glass and judge its quality in relation to the price asked. To buy wisely, take into consideration all the characteristics that fine American cut glass should have.

7.

EVALUATING CUT GLASS

AN APPRAISAL OF CUT GLASS INVOLVES TWO TYPES OF VALUES: PRICE AND quality. *Price* designates the dollars-and-cents cost of the item. Although learning to price cut glass with professional expertise is beyond the needs of most collectors, the collector does need at least to keep abreast of current prices in order to know whether a piece offered for sale is overpriced, fairly tagged, or underpriced (a sleeper). For example, in California we found sugar shakers priced from $95 to $135, but in the Midwest we saw one of comparable quality for $65 (Ills. 165 and 166).

Quality value refers to the special characteristics that make a piece of glass outstanding. The higher the quality of the item, the higher the price. So price and quality are interrelated but are not synonymous or interchangeable. Some collectors do place another value—a sentimental one—on their glass, especially if they have inherited it, searched a long time for certain wanted items, or feel attached to a certain pattern. These and other emotional reactions often prevent a collector from appraising his own cut glass objectively.

But even acknowledged experts in the field of cut glass will vary from 10 to 20 percent in setting a price on a piece of cut glass, although they will generally agree on the characteristics of a quality item. Consequently the collector—especially one who regards his collection as an investment—must learn to recognize quality characteristics. Consider these guidelines:

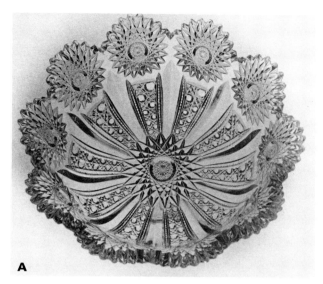

A

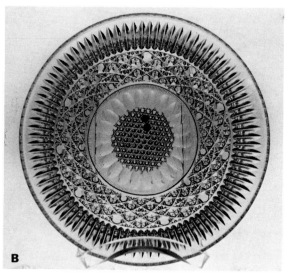

B

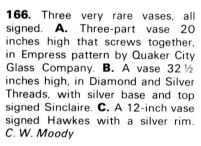

C

165. Three quality pieces, but only one is signed. **A.** Unsigned 11-inch bowl in hobstars and cane rays. *Tisnado Collection.* **B.** An 8-inch shallow bowl signed Libbey at the dots has a cane center, a band of thumbprints, Russian Canterbury, and a border of prism. **C.** Unsigned footed berry bowl in heavy cut. *Tisnado Collection*

166. Three very rare vases, all signed. **A.** Three-part vase 20 inches high that screws together, in Empress pattern by Quaker City Glass Company. **B.** A vase 32 ½ inches high, in Diamond and Silver Threads, with silver base and top signed Sinclaire. **C.** A 12-inch vase signed Hawkes with a silver rim. *C. W. Moody*

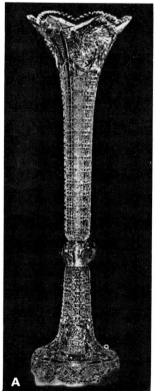

A

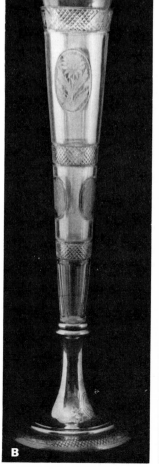

B

C

Standards of Quality

The quality of cut glass can range from the very poor to the museum piece. Some companies put out several grades of cut glass. For example, Pitkin and Brooks advertised a P & B grade that represented quality; their standard grade was said to equal that sold generally in the United States. They also sold imported glass, for which the company contracted with a foreign glasshouse for a cheaper cutting of Pitkin and Brooks designs.

Even companies with exceptional reputations for quality glass, such as Hawkes and Libbey, turned out cheaper pieces to meet the competition and to attract all types of customers; therefore each piece must be judged on its own merits.

The Blank

Evaluating a piece of cut glass begins with a study of the blank. As already explained, many companies bought blanks for cutting from such well-known glass firms as Dorflinger, Corning, Libbey, and Fry. Fry put out some of the finest blanks in his best period and some of the poorest in his late period.

A quality blank should have good luster. Quality cut glass has a blue-white, prismatic clarity because of its high lead content. With its high refractive index, lead crystal sparkles more than any other type of glass when cut and polished (Ill. 167). If a blank lacks this luster, it may be a figured or foreign blank. As previously discussed, grayness characterizes blanks blown in a mold or those made with more lime than lead. Some foreign glass—Canadian, for example—may need to be studied beside an American piece; the gray tint will then become more apparent.

167. Three 9-inch bowls that show luster in the glass. **A.** A bowl with unusual details of cutting. *George Clark.* **B.** Another bowl with a good blank for the cutting. *Argie Burwell.* **C.** The clarity of detail on this bowl shows a good blank and good cutting. *Evelyn Henzi*

132   Weight is another important criterion in judging cut glass. The lead content of the glass and the thickness of the blank make old American cut glass very heavy. An average 8-inch cut berry bowl will weigh 3 pounds; a cut pitcher 8 inches tall, around 6 pounds; a cut tumbler, about 10 ounces (Ills. 168 and 169). However, weight can be a deceptive factor too. Look for equal distribution of the weight in examining a piece. Items like tumblers, shot glasses, toothpick holders, and pitchers may have a weighted bottom—some of these have a base of solid glass an inch or more thick, but the walls are thin, the same from top to bottom, permitting only shallow cutting. The thick base supplies the weight.

168A. This 7-inch pitcher with strap handle clearly shows the thickness of the blank. *Hebel Collection.* **B.** Punch bowl signed Clark has an equally thick blank. *Walker Collection*

169. Two heavy pieces with very thick blanks. **A.** This 10-inch-high chalice punch bowl is signed Hawkes on top of the foot. *Tisnado Collection.* **B.** A 12-inch champagne pitcher. *Helen Breeding*

For example, if you clamp thumb and forefinger on either side of a good-quality tumbler and slide them downward, the wall of the piece thickens, beginning about an inch below the rim, for the deep cutting. Modern cut glass from Canada will have thin sides; the base of tumblers will be "loaded." On some modern compotes, it is the very thick base that provides the weight. Do not mistake a base of this kind for the old, ornate paperweight bases found on Brilliant cut glass.

Old Canadian glass cut on a lead blank differs little from the American. On the other hand, it is easy to detect the lighter weight of old Irish, Bohemian, and especially English glass.

When a piece of cut glass is balanced on the tips of the fingers and gently flicked with a fingertip, it gives a clear, bell-like tone. Quality cut glass gives a more resonant ring than ordinary crystal. The tone may range from a deep base to a sweet soprano note. Old flint glass and most modern lead crystal will also ring when given this test. The experienced collector learns to distinguish the different tones. The ring of new cut glass is either slightly flat or extremely high when compared to that of old cut glass. Many small articles such as individual salts, lidded dresser jars, and toothpick holders will not ring. Add to this list hinged boxes and stoppered or nearly closed pieces—decanters, cruets, rose bowls, and carafes. (Ills. 170 and 171)

170. Stoppered pieces will not ring. **A.** Whiskey jug in hobstar and cane squares has a lapidary stopper. *Aubright Collection.* **B.** Decanter in the Thistle pattern. *Doris Patterson.* **C.** Whiskey jug with matching stopper and triple-cut handle. *Argie Burwell*

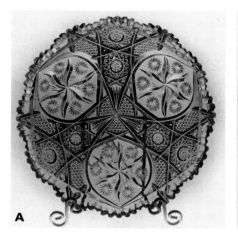

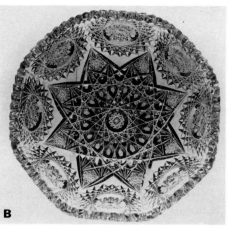

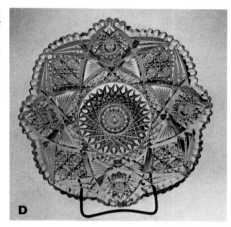

171. Bowls ring beautifully, the tone depending on the depth and size of the bowl. **A.** Even a small (7-inch) plate will ring if held correctly. *Patrick Curry.* **B.** This eight-sided bowl appears in two collections; it has a deep tone. *Evelyn Henzi and Thelma Prouse.* **C.** The size of a plate affects the ring. This one is 10 inches in diameter. *Tisnado Collection.* **D.** The ring of this 10-inch shallow bowl has less volume than that of a deeper bowl. *Rita Klyce*

The Pattern

Carefully examine every motif in the pattern of a piece of cut glass and fix it in your mind. Look for good balance in the design. The dominant motif should be repeated symmetrically in the overall design, as should the minor motifs. If the shape of the piece permits, the number of minor motif repetitions ordinarily equals the number of major ones. This matching of dominant and minor motifs may vary with handled pieces such as pitchers or with odd-shaped ones such as epergnes.

Minor motifs are often combined with the dominant one to form a star, intersecting circles, criss-crossing elipses, or overlapping diamonds. The design in each of these segments must balance perfectly for a quality piece. Even when two pieces have the same pattern, however, the number of segments depends on the size and shape of the piece. Most nappies have three segments and a bowl has four (Ill. 172).

The type of motif used is also important. A hobstar, for instance, in most cases indicates an older piece, and the choice of hobstar determines the quality of the item. The number of points does not necessarily influence the quality—an 8-point star can show as much quality as a 32-point star in some pieces. (As previously explained, a star may have any number of points, but most star points are multiples of four—equally spaced.) It is the center of the star that proves the quality. For the hobstar, the best center is a raised faceted star topped by a pyramidal one. An 8-point star may have a hobnail, diamond, or hobstar center (Ill. 173).

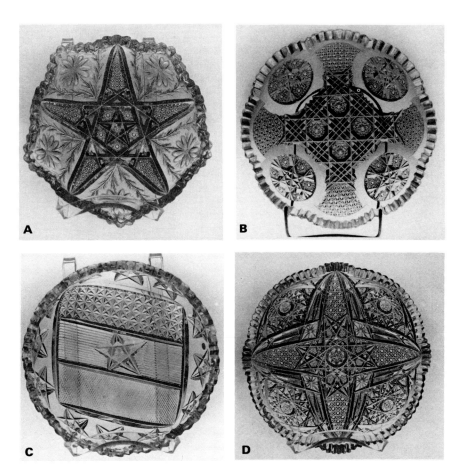

172. These bowls show good balance in design. **A.** A 7-inch bowl resembling the work of Tuthill. **B.** This bowl shows an unusually well-balanced design; it resembles the best work of Fry. *David Seiling.* **C.** An oddly planned arrangement that might have been made for some special event. **D.** An 8-inch bowl exhibiting rare balance in major and minor motifs.

173. Two large pieces that demonstrate excellent choices of motifs. **A.** A 12-inch tray with exceptionally detailed motifs that required much time to cut with such perfection. *Marie Hegarty.* **B.** A 14-inch tray on which a combination of geometric designs forms a flower. *George Clark*

Study the minor motifs, their intricacy of design in themselves and in combination with the major motif. Consider the amount of detailed cutting required to produce the pattern. Make sure the minor motif displays as intricate and skilled cutting as the dominant one. For example, a strawberry diamond contains more work than a simple crosshatching or a fan. But an excellently cut minor motif does not make up for a poorly done dominant one, nor does a good dominant motif hide an inferior minor one (Ill. 174).

A quality piece has sharply defined details. No matter how small the motif, every detail must be visible to the naked eye. For instance, a crosshatched button in the Russian pattern has a higher value than a clear one; but a button with a hobstar requires more detailed work. Clear and intricately cut details guarantee quality (Ill. 175).

A well-known named pattern such as Corinthian or Middlesex is another guarantee of quality. Some patterns proved so difficult to cut that major companies allowed only master craftsmen to work on them. Pieces with such patterns nearly always rate as fine quality. We have never seen such quality patterns as Lattice, Imperial, Parisian, or Arabian cut on any but quality blanks. Much top-quality cut glass, however, never had a name or number, as only the large companies published catalogs or secured patents.

The Cutting

To judge cutting, each piece has to be considered individually. The fact that a piece is marked Clark or Fry is no guarantee of quality—they both cut some very poor glass, too. The collector must check out certain specific characteristics on any piece in evaluating its cutting.

The first thing is to distinguish between sharpness and roughness. A poor polish or lack of smoothing will cause cutting to feel rough. On the other hand, acid polishing softens the sharp edges. Sharpness varies with the period of cutting, and so if the period of a piece can be established, that will give an indication of how sharp the cutting should be. Naturally, glass of the Brilliant Period feels the sharpest because the entire surface is cut.

Practice running the fingers over cut pieces, to learn to detect an acid polish, a figured blank, or a shallow cut—all these make the surface feel greasy. A quality item has a knifelike sharpness. Sometimes, however, a piece that is not so heavily cut may feel equally sharp and rate as a quality piece. During the Flower Period, the patterns and the use of figured blanks removed a great deal of the sharpness (Ill. 176).

A quality piece of cut glass requires a thick blank because of its deep cutting. Examine the rim of an item to gauge the thickness of the glass. The rims of most 9-inch bowls measure about ¾ inch in thickness. A compote, sugar or creamer, and other small items are about ½ inch thick. The cutter needed this depth for deep miters, faceted hobstars, and pinwheels (Ill. 177).

A quality item also shows accuracy in cutting; but the master craftsman worked freehand, and so on some pieces a fan may be longer than its matching counterpart or one star point shorter than another. Still, a master cutter was capable of great accuracy in cutting a design, and this accuracy marks a quality piece (Ills. 178 and 179).

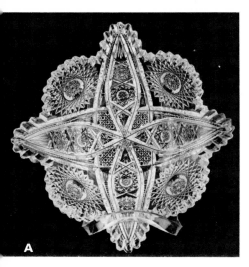

174. On these pieces the minor motifs are as well cut as the major ones. **A.** Square 8-inch bowl. *Aubright Collection.* **B.** A 7-inch signed Hawkes plate decorated with curved miters and hobstars. *Patrick Curry.* **C.** A 7-inch plate with beading accenting the diamonds separating the hobstars; signed Hawkes. *Patrick Curry.* **D.** An 8-inch plate cut about the same period as the other three. *Tisnado Collection*

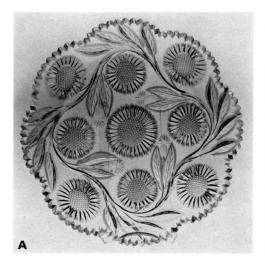

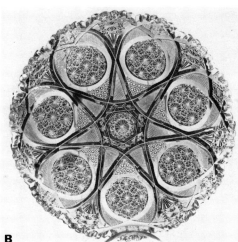

175. Two large plates and two bowls covered with intricate detail, with good balance maintained, are quality pieces. **A.** There is a rhythm to the sunflowers on this 12-inch plate. *Argie Burwell.* **B.** A 10-inch shallow bowl with a great deal of fine detail. *George Clark.* **C.** An 11-inch plate signed by Hawkes, obviously of museum quality. *Tisnado Collection.* **D.** This 9-inch bowl with hobstars accenting notched prisms is Nelson pattern, signed Hawkes and patented March 9, 1897. *Tisnado Collection*

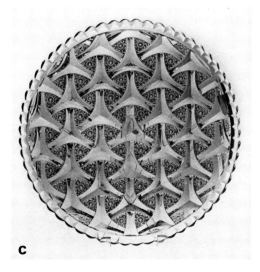

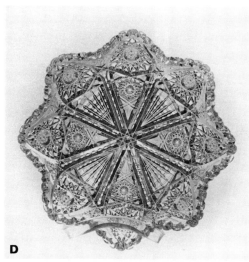

176. Three banana bowls and an ice cream platter that exhibit unusual sharpness in the cutting of detailed motifs. **A.** A rare bowl on a pedestal, 12 inches wide and 6 inches tall. *Patrick Curry.* **B.** An 11-inch banana bowl in Harvard and double-X lozenge. *Mrs. Jack Pelzner.* **C.** On this 11-inch banana bowl the cutter adapted the design to the shape. *George Clark.* **D.** Fine-cut details blend with the design of this 12 ½-inch ice cream platter in fishtail shape.

Two types of polishing have already been mentioned: by hand and with acid. The type can be determined by tilting the piece so that the light gives it a mirror look. Then the waviness of an acid polish will show. An acid-polished compote with a conical base sometimes shows graininess on the underrim, but—at times—the best acid-polishing work can hardly be detected. Then the collector must depend on feeling a piece to gauge its sharpness. With study and experience, the collector also soon learns the feel and look of quality pieces that

177. These quality pieces began with the thick blanks so necessary for good cutting. **A.** Heavily cut bowl on a pedestal with a teardrop. *George Clark.* **B.** A very rare two-part cake plate on a standard, 12 ½ inches wide and 8 ¾ inches high. *Patrick Curry.* **C.** Very unusual eggnog bowl on a base. *Tisnado Collection*

178. Two punch bowls in two parts on very heavy blanks. The bases can be used as compotes. **A.** *Tisnado Collection;* **B.** *Hebel Collection*

179. A 14-inch ice cream tray that shows great accuracy in cutting the deep pinwheels and hobstars. *Patrick Curry*

are buffed to a high degree of luster. A quality item has a mirror polish on all the uncut surfaces.

All these characteristics are aids that can help in determining the quality of a piece of cut glass. To determine exceptional quality, however, certain other unique features come into the picture.

Unique Features

If cut glass has one or more of the following additional features, its worth is substantially increased. (When quality increases, so does price.)

Variation in Form

Any time that a glass company varied a shape or made some addition to a standard design, the value of the piece increased. For example, the addition of a pedestal or base to an article required more work and increased the production cost. A pedestal includes both a stem and a base, such as appear on compotes, and so, as a rule, adding a pedestal cost more than adding only a base because of the extra work. If the pedestal on a piece had a decorated stem, that raised the cost still more. There were many ways of decorating a stem: twisting it, bulging it, adding a teardrop or two, squaring it, cutting notched flutes in it, or putting a ring around it. An especially tall compote or a square one is more unusual than one of average height (Ill. 180). (Incidentally, most authorities do not consider stemware as pedestal pieces; rather, the "pedestal" is an intrinsic part of the standard design.)

A

B

C

180. Three pieces on pedestals. **A.** An 8-inch-high compote with a flared bowl and hobstar cut base. **B.** Bowl, 9 inches high, on a pedestal; very sharply cut. **C.** A 9-inch compote with teardrop in the stem, which is cut with St. Louis diamonds. *George Clark*

181A. Pairs of cruets like these are rare because they have bases. **B.** The stopper of the wine decanter matches the body. *C.W. Moody*

A

B

If a piece ordinarily was made without a pedestal, the addition of one gives it a higher rating. We have seen pedestals on toothpick holders, a banana bowl, a berry bowl, cake plate, individual salts, and a sugar and creamer. A sugar and creamer on a tall pedestal rates higher than those on low standards. A teardrop enclosed in the pedestal further improves a piece, but not as much as a teardrop knob. (Ills. 154, 180)

On certain items, the glasshouse added only a base, but no stem. This increases the value if the item normally would not have had a base. Sometimes bases were added to wine decanters, water pitchers, cruets, and sugars and creamers. Most authorities consider a base on a vase as a standard design. A facet-cut knob on any piece adds a unique feature.

The type of cutting on the underside of a base or pedestal can add refinement. Although many standard pieces had a single star on the base, those of exceptional quality came with a 32-point hobstar or a group pattern. We have seen candlesticks with a Harvard base, a compote with Strawberry Diamond, a rosebowl with Russian, and a matchholder with Cane. A scalloped base adds a plus point too.

183. Pair of candlesticks with Harvard bases. *Hebel Collection*

182. Two wine decanters on pedestal bases. **A.** Decanter is 15 inches in height and has a steeple stopper. *Adolph F. Hansen.* **B.** This 10-inch liqueur decanter with a neck ring has notched flutes on the stopper. *George Clark*

184. Two or three handles add quality to an item. **A.** Double-handled mayonnaise bowl. *Tisnado Collection.* **B.** Double-handled ice bucket, 5 ½ inches high and 6 inches in diameter, has the added quality feature of a pedestal base. *Rita Klyce*

Handles upgrade a piece if that particular type of piece normally did not have them. Sugar bowls and creamers usually are handled pieces but compotes are not. Most nappies have no handles or only one.

Three handles on a nappy cost more to produce than two, but pieces with two handles rate above those with one handle or none. Likewise, triple-handled loving cups cost more than double-handled ones.

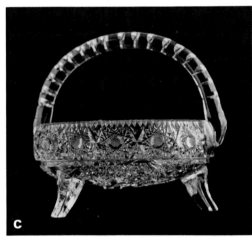
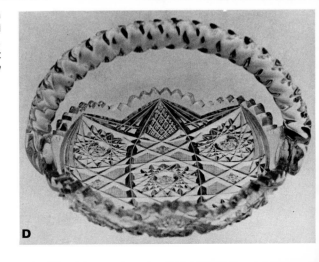

185. The cutting on the handle can add to the quality of a piece. **A.** The handle of this basket has a strawberry-diamond cut. *George Clark.* **B.** Basket handle here has a hobnail cut. *Hebel Collection.* **C.** The basket has a thumbprint handle, but it gains in quality because of its shape and the legs. *Helen Breeding.* **D.** Basket with a twisted handle.

A clear handle was the least expensive one to make. A handle becomes more elaborate according to whether it is decorated with one row of thumbprints, two rows, or even three. Flat handles with a pattern such as Harvard or Strawberry Diamond are rated even more desirable. We saw an unusual nappy handle decorated with notched rings, an added elaboration.

An unusual contour is a unique feature. A heart-shaped or clover-leaf nappy or one with the body extended to form a handle will have a higher appraisal than a plain round one. A fluted berry bowl, a square compote, a crescent compote, and an S-shaped celery boat all command higher estimates, as they are unique pieces of exceptional merit. A dish with double, triple, or quadruple divisions is also raised in appraisal. In fact, any deviation from the ordinary increases the rarity (Ill. 187).

Legs on a cake plate or a vase usually add value, but not the legs on a fernery—the standard fernery was always made with legs (Ill. 189).

Any special treatment of necks—the St. Louis diamond, the ringed neck, or the bulging neck characteristic of Libbey glass—adds a plus. It involved more work and so the cost was increased—in fact, the worth goes higher in proportion to the number of neck rings or bulges. A neck cut with St. Louis Diamonds, steps, or heavily notched flutes upgrades a piece still more.

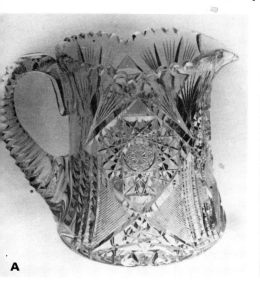

186. Two pitchers with unusual handles: **A.** A honeycombed handle. **B.** A cane cutting on the handle. *George Clark. Hebel Collection*

187. A rare shape also adds to the quality. An odd-shaped celery tray (**left**) in Notched Prism with hobstar base and a rare fluted bowl (**right**) signed Hawkes. We have seen only one other bowl like this.

188. Two sets of sugar and creamer. **A.** This set in Strawberry-Diamond is on a base. *Aubright Collection.* **B.** Footed set in buzz star.

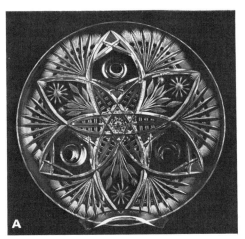

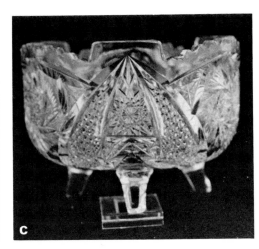

189. Legs do not add much quality unless the piece does not ordinarily have legs. **A.** Cake plate in Nassau pattern, signed Hoare on the rim. **B.** A fernery usually has legs. *Lucinda Baker Greiner.* **C.** Legs make this butter tub a rarity. *C. W. Moody*

Signatures

A signature on a piece of glass certainly raises the appraisal because it definitely identifies the company that cut the glass. A signature on high-quality glass, however, provides more merit than one on poor-quality pieces—after all, the presence of a signature never in itself guarantees the quality of a piece (Ill. 119).

Hawkes and Hoare used the same signature on all grades of cut glass, but Pitkin and Brooks usually signed only the top quality. The Libbey with a sword signature rates higher than a Libbey in a circle, a much later signature. To give a piece top rating, the signature must appear on high-quality glass.

Remember, too, that some companies cut better glass than others. For example, a signature by Tuthill, Libbey, or Hawkes rates higher than one by Unger, Hunt, or Irving. A general comparison of the glass produced by each company will verify this statement. Over the years, Tuthill, Libbey, and Hawkes signed more top-quality glass than the other three companies named. A number of companies may have cut quite average or below-average glass and yet produced one outstanding pattern; Royal pattern by Hunt is a good example.

Rarity

Rarity depends on a broad spectrum of characteristics. Probably the rarest pieces of all were those made as presentation pieces, on special order. Among these would be such items as decanters shaped like bowling pins, or a novelty baseball bat. Certain pieces with covers hold a close second place—lidded vegetable bowls and sugar bowls, for instance. Colored cut glass was made in such small quantities that it certainly deserves a rare rating, and a multicolored piece called rainbow ranks above a red or green cut-to-clear (Ill. 12). Certainly an excellent intaglio cut deserves a rare rating.

Glass lamps, heavily cut, have become a rarity because they were never cut in large quantities, were always costly, and many were broken. Of the numerous collections we photographed, five included a lamp. In the available catalogs from glass companies only Bergen illustrated a lamp. Several pictures of lamps in various styles appeared in catalogs from Marshall Field & Company, Oskamp, Nolting Company, and Higgins & Seiter. This scarcity of illustrations could imply that lamps were made only on special order.

Before the turn of the century the catalogs advertised kerosene lamps consisting of two ball-shaped pieces stacked on top of each other with a chimney in the upper one. Some companies even cut the chimney. Dealers and collectors refer to these as "Gone with the Wind" lamps. With the discovery of electricity, the catalogs advertised cut glass electroliers in three basic sizes. Most consisted of a flat or pointed mushroom-shaped top that dripped with crystal pendants. The 12- to 14-inch ones, often without pendants, contained a 6-inch dome and one light. Since these were used on a dresser in a bedroom, dealers refer to them as boudoir lamps. The middle size, 16 to 18 inches in height, contained one or two bulbs and had a 10-inch dome; an extra charge was made for the pendants. The tallest lamp varied in height from 22 to 30 inches and contained one or two bulbs, but pendants were optional. (Ill. 190.)

In the Flower Period companies used figured blanks and cut only flowers on lamps, or replaced the cut glass dome with a silk shade. Naturally these lamps do not come under the rare category. The catalogs that illustrate lamps use no other name than "lamp" or "electrolier."

Quality-cut miniatures and novelties certainly rank as rarities. Although these are sometimes referred to as salesmen's samples, the cutters we talked with said no such thing existed; the miniatures were either children's dishes, doll dishes, or items the cutters made just for fun. Whimseys, too, are uncommon—such objects as a paperweight shaped like a book, a card holder, and a salt shaker shaped like an egg. Museums now display these rarer pieces—e.g., the cut glass table and the St. Louis punch bowl at the Toledo Museum of Art.

A liner, particularly one of silver, adds rarity to an item. If the liner contains a signature, this adds further refinement. A high-quality matched set always commands a premium appraisal because it is unusual to find an entire set intact. For example, a wine decanter and its matching glasses or an ice cream platter with the matching plates would have a higher assessment as a complete set. We saw an exceptional set—a large ice cream platter and twelve matching nappies with handles—in Hawkes Chrysanthemum pattern that certainly qualified as a unique group.

By applying these standards and watching for unique features, you can add quality pieces to your collection. Likewise, you can use these guidelines to separate the quality items from the ordinary as you upgrade your collection.

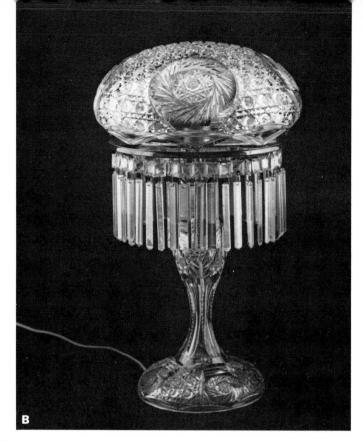

190. Four types of lamps that span the Brilliant Period. **A.** Intaglio-cut lamp, 18 inches tall, with both shade and base signed Tuthill. **B.** A 22-inch lamp in Harvard pattern with added pinwheel motifs. **C.** A 20-inch lamp with hobstars added to Notched Prism pattern signed Fry on base and shade. *Aubright Collection.* **D.** Dating late in the Brilliant Period is this lamp with cut base in Middlesex by Hawkes and a silk shade.

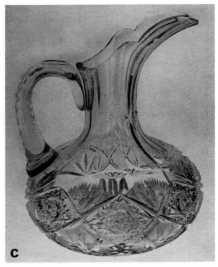

191A. This covered dish, 9 inches in diameter, qualifies as a rarity. **B.** Most hinged boxes are rare, as is this one in Libbey's Florence pattern. **C.** A pitcher with a rare shape, deeply cut on a heavy blank. *C. W. Moody*. **D.** Rare picture frame signed Hawkes.

192. Novelties, whether large or small, are rare. **A.** Miniature two-handled bowl. **B.** Paperweight shaped like a book in Russian pattern, cut at Corning Glass Works by Frank Schosger. *Irma Adams*. **C.** Card holder in Harvard. *Adolph F. Hansen*

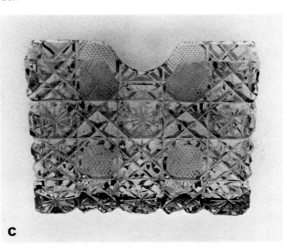

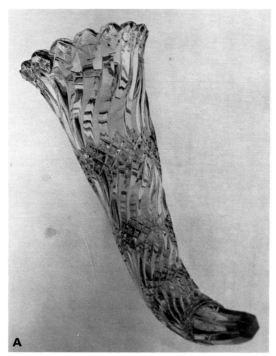

193A. A rare cornucopia vase. **B.** A 12-inch epergne. *Rita Klyce.*
C. Drapery tiebacks. *Patrick Curry*

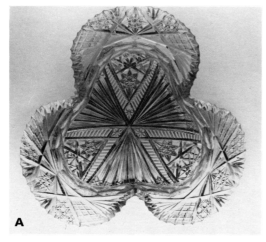

194A. Top view of a spittoon. *David Seiling.* **B.** Another spittoon, signed Pitkin & Brooks on the rim.

195. Four collector's items. **A.** Flower center with an upper section that lifts out. **B.** Two-part powder box signed on both pieces by Hawkes. **C.** Heavily cut champagne bucket. *Aubright Collection.* **D.** Nappy with thumbhold; heavily cut but unsigned.

196A. Full-size water pitcher with an ice guard. *Argie Burwell.* **B.** Invalid's pitcher is 6 ½ inches in height. *George Clark.* **C.** Wineglass with silver base signed Shreve is exceptionally rare. *C. W. Moody.* **D.** A true novelty piece, 6 inches high and signed Hawkes. *Rita Klyce*

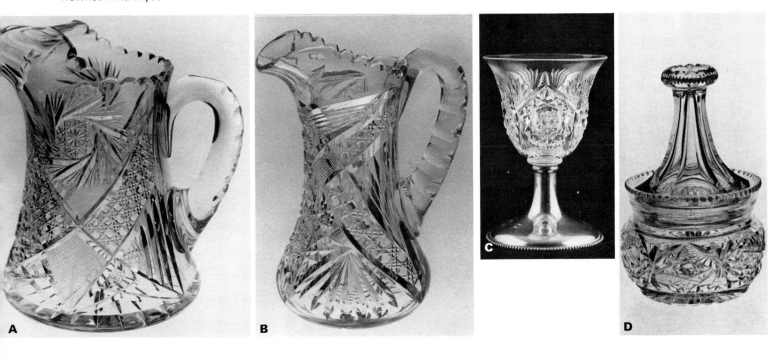

Comparative Pricing

Putting a dollar value on a collection takes considerable study and long experience in dealing with cut glass—more than most collectors have or want to have. However, through *comparative pricing*—averaging the prices set by various sources—the collector can determine a reasonable price for a piece of cut glass in a specified area.

Annual price guides are a compilation of prices customers have actually paid for articles. Collectors and dealers often disagree, sometimes violently, with these guides, and they do have some drawbacks. They can list only a limited number of items and well-known patterns; they cannot cover the entire range of quality for all cut glass items, for instance, nor list the variation in prices according to all geographical areas. Price guides do, however, provide a starting point for comparison with dealers' prices in the collector's own area.

Some antiques shop owners and dealers who specialize in cut glass and have a broad experience can price better than the guides. Generally, in setting a price, a dealer considers the quality, the quantity, and the market demand. Some dealers set the price for an item a certain percentage above what they paid for it regardless of its quality. Sleepers are most likely to be found at the establishments of such dealers. Others who handle very little cut glass rely on the better-known price guides. A few fall in love with an item and price it so high that no one will buy it and take it away. A visit to several shops will make clear the average prices in an area.

Attending an antique show where a good deal of cut glass is exhibited offers a valuable source of price information as well as a saving in time. Here, again, there are several factors to be considered. A dealer who sees a competitor with higher prices than his own may proceed to raise his prices. Also, often an inexperienced dealer who has put a reasonable price on his merchandise, based on what it cost him, finds other dealers buying out his entire stock before the show opens; dealers who have few opportunities to buy from private owners buy instead from one another. Each time a piece is sold—from one dealer to another—the new owner takes a profit, until finally the price goes well beyond the actual value. Furthermore, some dealers automatically raise all their prices to offset the cost of entering a show. Consequently, private individuals who want to sell their cut glass get a false idea of its value when they see the inflated prices at some shows. We have noticed the same items returning, year after year, to the same show with the same dealer, the price becoming a bit higher at each successive show. Hence, a high price does not necessarily indicate true value or quality. Check now long an item remains unsold before you accept its price as a true evaluation.

In our experience, collectors generally place a very realistic value on their cut glass. They will confide what they paid and whether they consider the cost too high or just reasonable, or sometimes that an item was a genuine "sleeper." The beginning collector will profit by getting to know other collectors in the same area and discussing prices with them. They have come by their knowledge from a combination of price guides, antiques shops, shows, and discussions with other collectors.

Prices paid at auctions have skyrocketed above those in antiques shops. A number of dealers we have talked with seem to think that amateurs or collectors do most of the buying at auctions. In spite of the generally high prices at auctions today, however, occasionally there is a sale where few of the customers are greatly interested in cut glass, and at such an auction cut glass prices are usually quite moderate. Because of this fluctuation, auction prices alone do not offer a sound basis on which to evaluate a collection.

Within the last five years several antiques tabloids have come on the market, and there are dealers who sell only by mail through advertisements in these papers. Reading the advertisements and noting the prices listed can be very enlightening for the collector, but the address of the advertiser should also be considered. In some areas collectors prefer pattern or art glass, and cut glass may sell for less than it does elsewhere. In areas where there is great interest in cut glass, the price is higher.

In these antiques papers, recently there has been a trend away from listing the price of items pictured in the advertisements and in accounts of shows; to learn the price, the reader must either call or write to the dealer. Some dealers offer to send a price list of items if the reader provides a self-addressed stamped envelope (SASE). By all means send for such lists. They can prove helpful, although a piece must be seen for its true quality to be gauged.

Using all the above-mentioned sources, any collector can easily make up his own price guide. Here is an example of the procedure: Suppose you want to check the value of a two-handled divided nappy (Ill. 197). Begin with the usual price for a single-handled nappy of similar quality, by checking the prices in antiques shops and shows, talking with collectors, studying price guides, attending auctions, and examining the advertisements in antiques papers and magazines. Eventually you will be able to establish the average price of a single-handled nappy.

If your two-handled divided nappy is a quality piece, start adding percentages to the average price of a single-handled nappy. For the two handles and the division into sections, add 20 percent to the base price. For the presence of a top signature, add 10 percent to the base price; for color or intaglio cutting, add 20 percent. In the same manner, deduct 20 percent if the cutting was done on a figured blank. For an acid-polished piece, deduct 10 percent. Make comparable deductions for damage or any defects. Following this procedure will enable you to make an educated guess much as the so-called authorities do. Soon you will be able to put a fairly accurate value on any piece.

197. Scarcity makes an item rare. **A.** Two-handled nappy with buzz stars and hobstars. *Patrick Curry.* **B.** Sinclaire signed this clock; the works are by Spawling & Company, Chelsea Works, Chicago.

By keeping a record of the price paid for an item and also periodically checking current prices, you can determine any change in price for each piece in your collection. If you have observed quality standards in your buying and kept up with comparative pricing, you yourself can estimate the dollar value of your collection at any time with little trouble, and furthermore you will know the amount to ask if you decide to sell or trade a piece. If you apply for insurance on your collection, having this record of price information available for the one who appraises it will also reduce the amount of time he has to spend on the appraisal.

8.

HELPFUL TIPS
FOR THE COLLECTOR

IN THE BEGINNING, A COLLECTION OF CUT GLASS USUALLY CONSISTS OF the more plentiful pieces such as bowls, nappies, relishes, small plates, and similar items. As the collector gains experience, however, he begins to want the more unusual pieces (Ills. 198 and 199). Where does he find these? In fact, what are the best sources for good cut glass of the Brilliant Period, in general?

We have combined our experiences with those of others, in order to provide some guidelines on collecting that may prove helpful, especially to the beginner. The collector who has pursued cut glass as a hobby for several years has probably already established profitable sources of supply, but both the novice and the experienced collector may have overlooked some of the following possibilities.

The first of these is flea markets, which are of two types—permanent ones open regularly on weekends or sporadic ones sponsored by clubs, churches, or various civic organizations as fund-raising ventures. The second type offers better possibilities for finding "sleepers." At either type of flea market, it is a good idea to shop with the one-timers or the ground-spreaders—these are often people moving to smaller living quarters who want to get rid of some of their possessions, heirs who have no use for what they have inherited, or collectors upgrading their collections. Strike up a conversation with the seller and determine his motive for selling. I met a woman who had brought only a few cut glass bowls and nappies to the flea market, but she invited me to her home to buy choicer pieces. (Ill. 200)

A

B

C

198. Here are some unusual pieces attractive to collectors. **A.** Tobacco jar, 8¾ inches in height. *Rita Klyce.* **B.** Captain's cruet signed Hawkes. *Roy Brown.* **C.** Oddly shaped catsup bottle with a mushroom stopper. *George Clark.* **D.** Sachet bottle in hobstar and fan. *George Clark*

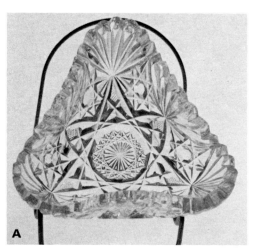

A

D

199. Interesting small pieces add variety to a collection. **A.** A triangular nappy signed Hawkes, in an 8-point star motif. *Walker Collection.* **B.** Handled mustard, quite rare. *George Clark.* **C.** Heart-shaped nappy, bought at a flea market.

B

C

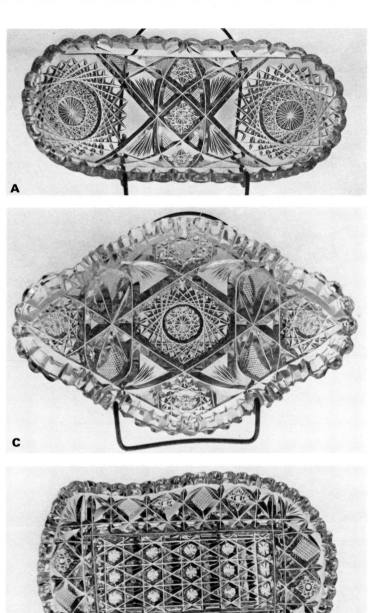

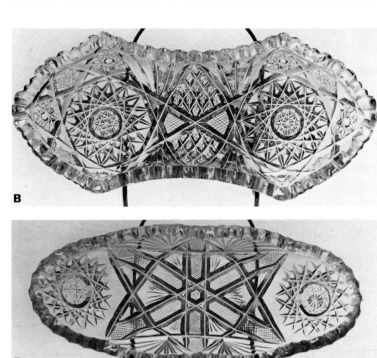

200. Some very good cutting and varied shapes can be found in relish dishes. **A.** A 7-inch relish dish with 24-point hobstars deeply cut. *Marie Hegarty.* **B.** Its odd shape and heavy cutting in a pattern similar to Libbey's Empress made this a good buy at a garage sale. **C.** The shape, the heavy blank, and the excellent balance of the pattern made this piece a sleeper at an auction. **D.** Although unsigned, this 7-inch relish dish is cut in the Florence pattern by Hoare. **E.** This relish dish is on a Bergen blank, as seen in the Bergen catalog, and the style of cutting also indicates a Bergen piece. *Patrick Curry.* **F.** The shape and the deeply cut hobstars make this a very good piece. *Irma Adams*

201. A glove box 10½ inches long bought at a garage sale. *Sharalyn Spiteri*

155

156 A garage sale can be, in essence, a mini flea market—sometimes several individuals may get together and advertise a one-day sale. Here there may be bargains. One woman disposed of an entire estate by running a garage sale. Look for those sales that advertise antiques, and always inquire whether the seller has any cut glass for sale that is not displayed. At one garage sale a friend of ours asked about cut glass, and the woman brought a glove box from inside her home and sold it at a bargain price (Ill. 201).

Many flea markets, rummage, or garage sales have nappies, bowls, vases, and other pieces that were produced in abundance, and the prices are generally lower than in shops. Sometimes the prospective buyer can try making an offer or asking the seller for a discount—whether the seller will bargain is usually quite apparent. Avoid haggling, however; buy or forget it.

202. Some collectors look for small individual pieces. **A.** An individual olive dish bought at an estate sale because of its detailed cutting and good blank. **B.** An individual nut tray, 4½ inches, with the same minute cutting as that found on a larger piece. *George Clark.* **C.** Individual olive dish bought at an auction, with buzz stars and a band of strawberry diamonds. **D.** This olive dish, which came from a flea market, is part of a collection of small items. **E.** A 5-inch nut tray with a hobstar and diamonds. *George Clark.* **F.** Rare miniature signed Hawkes. *George Clark*

Antiques shows offer three advantages: some of the dealers present usually specialize in cut glass; the collector has an opportunity to talk with knowledgeable people, and also a chance to check the prevailing prices. The large dealers who occupy the choice locations at a show and who often sell cut glass exclusively know how to price. Since they bring high-quality and rare items as leaders, to attract attention, it is worthwhile to study their displays. These dealers have the most-wanted and the hard-to-find pieces, but you will pay full price for them. In the fringe area are smaller dealers who handle only a few items of cut glass but may have a real "sleeper." Such dealers handle both quality and mediocre items.

Always at least *ask* for a better price, particularly on an expensive item or when purchasing several pieces. Sometimes prices are reduced at the end of a show, depending on whether the dealer has had good or poor sales; the prices in his shop may be more moderate than those in a show, so it can be worthwhile to visit the shop of any dealer who displayed quality glass at a show. By all means, make friends with the cut glass dealers and give them a list of the hard-to-locate items you want.

When staying even briefly in an unfamiliar town, telephone the antiques shops listed in the yellow pages and ask about their stock of cut glass. Often a dealer will volunteer information about others who specialize in cut glass. The antiques dealers association in some cities supplies a map of the locality listing the antiques shops, but only those belonging to the association. Other directories of shops are also available—the National Association of Dealers in Antiques, Inc., publishes one, as do various state organizations and antiques magazines. Some antiques shops sell small booklets listing dealers in specific areas, such as the Western United States.

Real treasures in cut glass can turn up in the most unlikely places, and so no possible source should be overlooked. One such source is "unclaimed storage." People sometimes leave things in metropolitan storage warehouses until the storage bill exceeds the value of the articles, so the owners forfeit their possessions or conveniently forget them. (Some items are left so long that they turn into antiques!) Such articles are put into display rooms and offered for sale. In the past, we have found several bargains in unclaimed storage sales, but recently the prevailing prices almost equal those in antiques shops.

Auction sales are another source for cut glass. The collector who cannot attend the actual auction may attend the preview and leave a written bid for any piece that interests him. Lately, bidding for cut glass has grow so spirited that auction prices sometimes exceed the actual cash value of the pieces.

Cut glass is frequently advertised in antiques magazines. Anyone who buys glass by this method needs to have a clear understanding as to the condition of the piece and the terms of the sale: for example, can the article be returned if the buyer is not satisfied? Most magazines carefully check their advertisers, and so if the merchandise is not as advertised, the buyer should send a complaint to the magazine.

Sometimes the heirs of an estate will hold a sale directly on the estate property. They may hire appraisers to set the prices and do the selling themselves, or have the entire sale handled by a company that makes a business of dispersing estates. When the prices are set by a nonprofessional, there may be some bargains in both cut glass and other categories at an estate sale (Ills. 207 and 208).

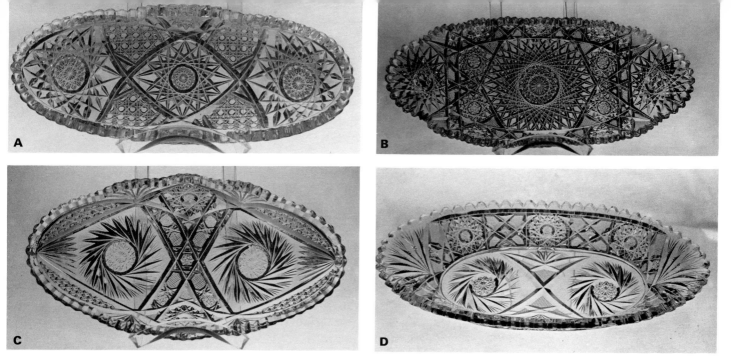

203. Every collection needs a bread tray. **A.** An 11-inch tray that could double for a celery tray, with cane and hobstar motifs. *Ann Dunlap.* **B.** Heavily cut 13-inch tray with 32-point hobstars. **C.** A 14-inch bread tray has buzz stars and a band of Harvard pattern. *Rita Klyce.* **D.** Deeper bread tray with hobstars, a crosshatched band, and buzz stars in the base. *Mrs. Jack Pelzner*

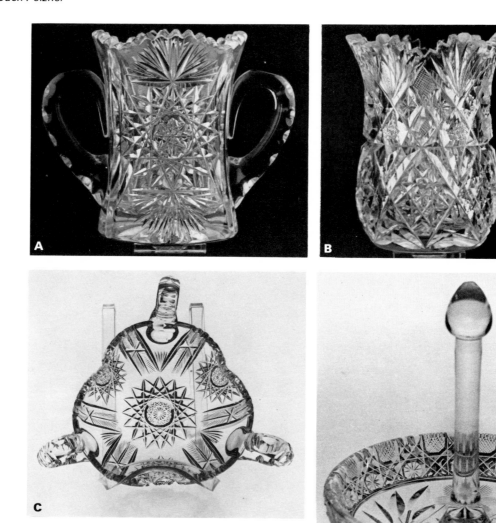

204. These items might well appear on a collector's "wanted" list: **A.** Two-handled spooner with hobstars and fans. **B.** An upright spooner on a thick blank, with minute cutting. **C.** Three-handled nappy with hobstars and blaze cutting. *George Clark.* **D.** A stick dish with flowers and Harvard band.

205. Most collections have a pitcher or two. **A.** An 8-inch water pitcher cut in Strawberry-Diamond with buzz stars. **B.** Tankard pitcher with 24-point hobstars. *George Clark.* **C.** Cereal pitcher in Hoare's Creswick. **D.** A 12-inch pitcher with flashed stars. **E.** Pitcher decorated with bull's-eyes and diamond hobstars. *C. W. Moody.* **F.** Milk pitcher with hobstars and miters. *Don Carr*

206. Heart-shaped pieces were cut in many designs. **A.** Heart-shaped nappy in Heart pattern by Pitkin & Brooks. *Adolph F. Hansen.* **B.** This heart has the notched prism motif around a hobstar. *Patrick Curry.* **C.** Heart bought at a warehouse sale.

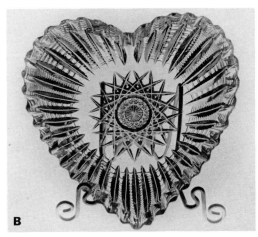
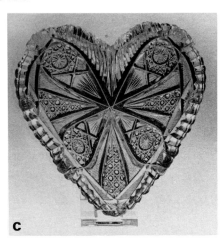

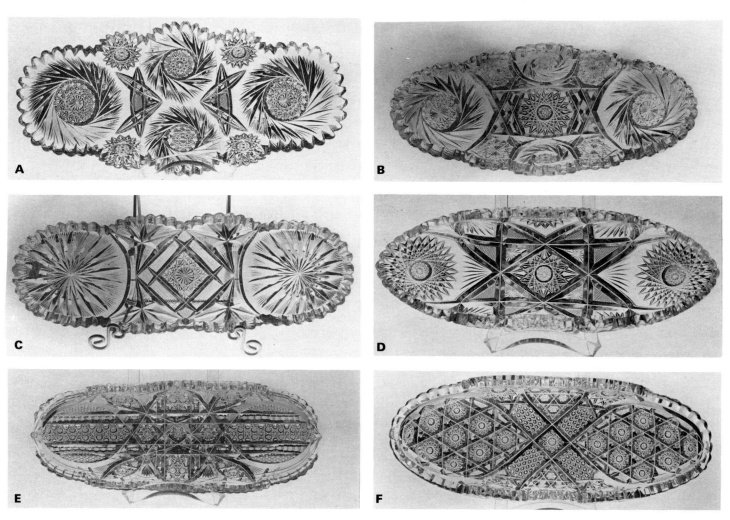

207. The shape of the celery tray inspired some unusual patterns. **A.** Pinwheels characteristic of Clark dominate this 11-inch celery tray. *Rita Klyce.* **B.** On this 10-inch tray buzz stars spin around a hobstar center. **C.** The sunburst motif seems to explode from the design of this tray. *Patrick Curry.* **D.** The crosshatching and hobstar base will keep bruises from showing on this 12-inch tray. *Eleanor Lovett.* **E.** An unusual band of hobnails topped with hobstars makes this 12-inch tray outstanding. *Irma Adams.* **F.** Clusters of hobstars and bands of the cane motif on this celery tray strongly suggest Egginton. *Jean Rieth*

208. Bowls made the perfect wedding or anniversary gift. **A.** An 8-inch bowl with nailhead diamonds covering the area between the miters. **B.** This 9-inch bowl has rhythmic miter cutting. **C.** A 9-inch bowl with a five-fluted shape. *Don Carr.* **D.** Another 9-inch bowl, with simplicity of design, signed Clark. *C. W. Moody*

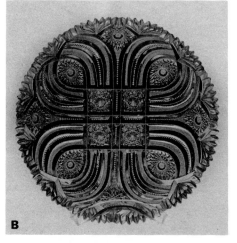

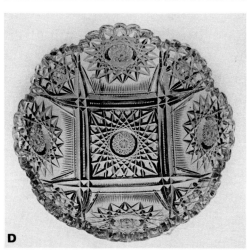

Collectors with imagination and initiative have also found quality cut glass by unusual means. One of our acquaintances used to spend Sunday afternoons on pleasant days driving around neighborhoods of old homes. If he saw someone in a yard, he would stop and ask if the person owned any cut glass and wanted to sell it. Even if he got a negative answer, sometimes the person would refer him to neighbors or friends who might want to sell their cut glass. Another collector advertises her desire to buy cut glass in small town newspapers a day or two before she arrives in the area. She has found several pieces of colored cut glass this way. A very ingenious collector has discovered that small shops in retirement neighborhoods frequently accept cut glass in trade for food and other supplies. In one such area, a florist exchanged flowers for cut glass, which he sold to a friend of ours .

By all means let others know that you collect cut glass. We have found that word of mouth works very well. Friends may tell you of a widow or widower moving from a large home into a condominium or of a person wanting help on an estate sale. Open your eyes and ears, run up your antennae, and you'll discover other possible sources to investigate in hunting for rich cut glass treasures.

209. Finding wine decanters with handles may take considerable search. **A.** This 10-inch decanter has 8-point stars in a cross-hatched background typical of Hoare. *Marie Hegarty.* **B.** A 12-inch one signed Libbey. *Aubright Collection*

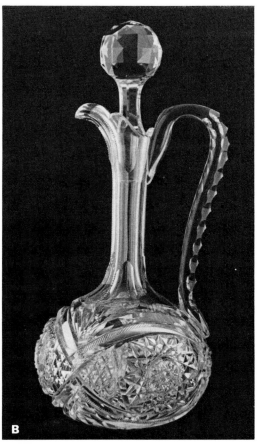

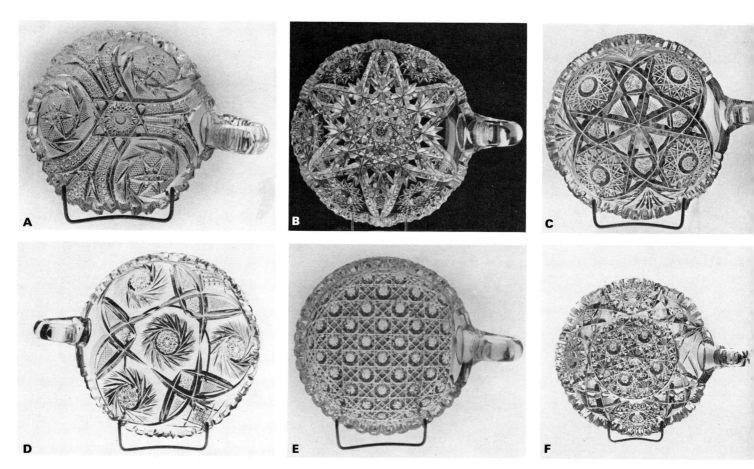

210. With so many 6-inch cut nappies available to choose from, the collector must become a discriminating buyer. **A.** On this nappy, 6-point stars in a diamond background form the center of the buzz. *George Clark.* **B.** This nappy in Expanding Star pattern appears in two collections. **C.** A nappy cut in 16-point hobstars that appears in four collections. **D.** Nappy showing rhythm cutting with buzz stars. *Alice Peri.* **E.** Nappy cut by Sterling. *C. W. Moody.* **F.** Nappy in Royal pattern by Hunt. *George Clark*

Care of Glass

Cut glass requires no more care than any other fine antique. Most collectors and dealers agree, however, on certain general procedures. For example, cut glass needs to be washed periodically. Using any good detergent and warm water, make a suds in a plastic tub or container, and scrub the pieces with a soft-bristle brush such as a vegetable brush, toothbrush, or nail brush. Rinse them thoroughly in water of the same temperature, drain on a Turkish towel, and then dry with a soft lint-free towel or paper towels. Many West Coast dealers wash cut glass with a product called Crystal Wash, which gives glass an excellent sparkle, almost seeming to place a coating on it so that merely dusting the pieces brings back their sparkle. No doubt other areas have similar products that work better than ordinary detergents. The less often cut glass is washed, the better—any handling, especially of slippery wet glass, increases the risk of damaging or breaking it.

To remove sediment from vases, cruets, and decanters, pour in some water and add a pellet-type denture cleaner; let soak over night. If this does not dislodge the sediment, put water in the piece and add three tablespoonfuls of a presoak detergent used in washing clothes (perhaps Axion); let soak for several days. (For smaller pieces, use proportionately less powder.) After the soaking, loosen the sediment with a long, cotton-tipped swab. The operation may have to be repeated several times or the soaking time increased.

Never use ammonia or a strong bleach in cleaning cut glass—either one may cause it to deteriorate and become sick. Make sure to let the insides of decanters, bottles, and cruets dry thoroughly by turning them upside down in a plastic rack for several hours. If the stopper is put in before the piece is thoroughly dry, a white stain will appear. Needless to say, cut glass should not be washed in a dishwasher, since it should not be subjected to extremes of either heat or cold. Also avoid placing it in strong sunlight or using cut glass pieces to store food in a refrigerator.

Like most other collections, a collection of cut glass must be seen to be enjoyed—there is little satisfaction or pleasure in owning something that must be kept hidden away out of sight. Display your cut glass in any type of cabinet with glass doors, and locate the cabinet in a place with fairly even temperatures. Take care not to stack one piece inside another, in order to avoid scratching or chipping the glass.

Pieces like vases and a punch bowl or epergne can be put on a table or buffet to enhance the decor of a room. Most collectors like to use certain items regularly—a couple of bowls, a water pitcher, compotes, sugar and creamer, or nappies; these can be kept in a handy spot in the dining area, perhaps in a breakfront (Ills. 211 and 212). A cut glass jewel box, pomade or vaseline jars, powder boxes, and cologne bottles lend a touch of elegance to dresser or dressing table.

Avoid placing any piece of cut glass where someone is likely to brush against it and knock it off. Study the traffic patterns of your home and avoid positioning glass near the busy routes.

211. A large punch bowl requires adequate display space. This one has five shooting stars in the design. *Walker Collection*

212. Pieces used frequently need to be stored where easily accessible. **A.** A 7-inch plate with alternating shooting stars and hobstars. **B.** A 7-inch plate with hobstar border. **C.** This 9-inch bowl makes fruit salad look especially delicious; it is signed Egginton. *Marie Hegarty.* **D.** Calling card tray, a good conversation piece. **E.** A 7-inch shallow bowl signed Clark. **F.** A 6-inch plate with hobstars and a cluster center.

Repairs

Sometimes the collector will come upon a magnificent but damaged piece that an expert glass cutter could restore to mint condition by recutting the rim to remove chips or flakes. Make sure such a piece has enough clear border so that the cutter need not cut into the design. On a thick blank, occasionally he can grind out a flake or cut a design over it. For example, he can remove a flake on the lip of a pitcher or the rim of a bowl or vase quite easily, but on thin glassware only the slightest of flakes can be removed (Ill. 213).

An expert polishing will remove heavy bruises—even those that look milky white or have the appearance of serious damage. In our collection is a shallow Corinthian pattern bowl signed Libbey in which someone evidently had arranged flowers, using a heavy metal frog that bruised the glass very badly. For only a nominal fee, a glass company polished and restored the mirror finish.

Most urban areas have glass experts who can do work of this kind. Ask for information about such an expert artisan from a glass company or from local antiques dealers who sell cut glass. Some cutters will accept glass to repair only if it is carried in by hand; others advertise in antiques magazines that pieces needing repairs can be sent by mail. In any case, the cutter assumes no responsibility for breakage—the collector must accept that risk.

165

Do not knowingly ever buy a cracked piece. If you have a cracked item, any clear epoxy glue on the market can seal off the crack or mend it if it breaks. A glass restorer may even fill in missing chips so beautifully that the mend will not be noticed by the casual observer although it is readily apparent on closer observation. A glass restorer told me she could put a coat of clear glue over a fracture to reinforce it, but that this would not hide the break.

Most metropolitan areas also have companies that resilver plated parts worn with use. Some ask that you remove the silver fitting from the glass, but others will remove it themselves. Removing silver fittings from a piece of cut glass requires patience and time. Place the item in a container and cover it completely with warm water. Let it soak until the water is cool; *gently* move the piece back and forth. If the fitting does not come loose, repeat the process. Each soaking loosens some of the plaster so that eventually the silver will separate from the glass. The person who does the plating generally will put the fitting back in place, but the collector can also do this quite easily with plaster of Paris. Coat the inside of the silver with plaster, leaving room for inserting the rim of the glass. Slip the silver fitting in place over the glass, remove any excess plaster, and let set for twenty-four hours for the plaster to harden.

Some experts can remove the cloudy type of sickness from a piece with a narrow neck by using a very strong acid and working with protective safety equipment. Other specialists can polish sick glass if they can easily reach the area that is affected. A man in Upland, California, has invented a tool that will go through a narrow neck and then spread out to do the polishing. Most of these experts charge a set fee for their efforts regardless of whether or not they succeed. They also do not guarantee that the sick appearance will not return.

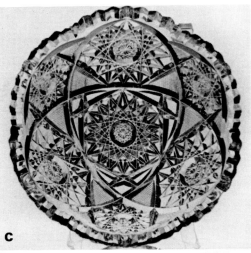

213A. On the nappy shown here, the design is so close to the rim that if chips had to be removed, the repair would cut into the pattern. This is a point to consider in buying a damaged piece. **B.** A rather unusual triangular nappy. *Rita Klyce.* **C.** This nappy, bought at a flea market, has had the rim completely recut to remove numerous chips.

Parting Advice

Whenever we meet collectors, we always ask them what advice they can give that would be helpful to others. Most of them have sad tales to relate about their experiences that usually end with: "If I had known then what I know now!" The following advice may be useful:

Experienced collectors warn that pieces of cut glass should be chosen in keeping with the available display area. Small pieces are suitable for the person who must keep his collection in a moderately sized cabinet or two. More sizable items that can be shown off to advantage only on a big buffet or sideboard are better accommodated in a home with larger rooms. In any case, the cut glass on display should add a note of elegance but not make a home look like a museum.

The serious collector should make it his business to keep up with all the books published on his subject. Getting acquainted with the local public library is a good idea—you can decide which books on cut glass you want to buy and have on hand for ready reference, and examine a wide variety of antiques magazines as well. Local libraries are also able to secure additional material on loan from museums and historical associations, if a subscriber requests it.

Most collectors subscribe to several antiques magazines. Choose those that seem to publish articles on glass quite frequently and to list antiques shows. The show announcements and dealers' advertisements may list available pieces of cut glass. These magazines also review new books and mention old catalog reprints for sale. Any time you see a reprint of an old catalog advertised, buy yourself a gift.

Whenever you travel, research the area along your route so that you will not miss museums and glass collections. The Toledo Museum of Art in Toledo, Ohio, has a display of Libbey glass and old catalogs. Corning Museum in Corning, New York, also has glass displays and offers a good deal of information on Hawkes and some on Hoare. Various museums and libraries in other parts of the country specialize in the work of other famous glass artisans such as Dorflinger and Fry.

As already recommended in these pages, take advantage of any opportunity to talk with dealers who sell cut glass and with collectors. Most of these people have accumulated valuable knowledge through experience and word of mouth. One dealer who specializes in signed pieces pointed out to me unusual places to look for signatures; another gave me much basic information on Canadian glass. Anyone who deals in cut glass or collects it can almost always help authenticate an old piece or contribute new information.

Another bit of good advice for the collector is to make a list of the various items desirable to add to his collection. This may include items needed to complete a set or a piece to replace a broken one, as well as pieces the collector particularly wants to own. We started to collect matching sets, and now have a dozen clarets, wines, sherries, cordials, and water tumblers. Eventually we hope to find the matching goblets. You may want to accumulate a set of matching small plates, butter pats, or nut dishes, or perhaps concentrate on olive dishes or other small pieces (Ills. 216 and 217).

214. These items are easily displayed in a cabinet or whatnot: **A.** Perfume bottle 4 inches tall. **B.** Smelling salts bottle in Chrysanthemum by Hawkes. **C.** A 4½-inch sugar shaker. *David Seiling.* **D.** Squat mustard pot.

215. Some collectors specialize in bowls or plates: **A.** An 8-inch bowl on a figured blank with rather odd flowers. **B.** A 12-inch plate with another type of flower on a figured blank. *Tisnado Collection.* **C.** A 12-inch plate with a flashed star in the center and a band of hobstars. *Tisnado Collection.* **D.** This 10-inch plate has a hobstar band and a flower center. *Tisnado Collection*

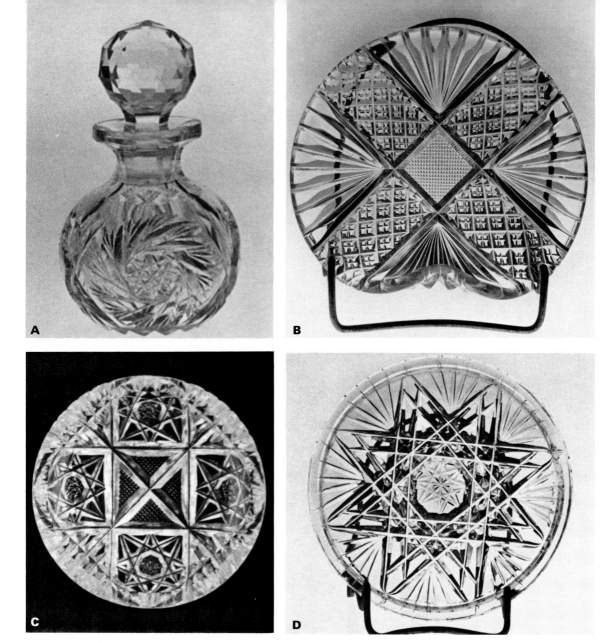

216. Small pieces offer interesting variety. **A.** Perfume bottle, 2 ½ inches tall. **B.** A rare item, a pin tray. **C.** Water coaster signed Fry. **D.** Butter pat with 8-point star. *George Clark*

Sometimes the collector will have an odd sugar or creamer from a broken set. We have several of these, and we carry along pictures of them and any other items we want to match whenever we go to a flea market or antiques shop or show, nearby or away from home. We have matched two sugar and creamer sets in this way and hope to match more. To find tops for salt and pepper shakers or stoppers for bottles and cruets, the piece itself should be taken along.

Our list of most-wanted items began with a wine decanter, a whiskey jug, a syrup pitcher, a whiskey bottle, and a cake plate, and we have found all of them. Do not, however, take the first example you see of an item on your list; look for a quality piece. In fact, any time you find a quality item at a good price, buy it. And don't let your list blind you to a sleeper. Finding a sleeper adds excitement to collecting.

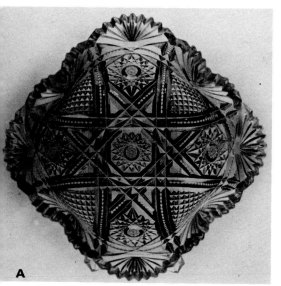

217. Here are additional items that might go on a "wanted" list. **A.** Square dish with diamonds and hobstars. **B.** Deeply cut water carafe with a decorated neck for a good grip. *Jean Rieth.* **C.** A covered butter dish. *Rita Klyce.* **D.** Cookie jar, 8½ inches in height, with good balance in its design and detailed cutting.

An important aspect of collecting is continually upgrading your collection. Too many owners become sentimental about the glass they own and refuse to upgrade. Always emphasize quality—not quantity—in your collection. Replace an item with a better piece; then sell the first one or—better still—trade it.

Dealers can often sell a small piece faster than they can a larger and more expensive item. Any time you see a quality piece of cut glass that is underpriced, buy it and trade it to a dealer for something you want, or make a trade with another collector (Ills. 218-219).

A collector can compile his own list of buyers. Antiques classes offer one potential market, but also be alert for buyers when you go to a lunch, cocktail party, or club meeting. When you decide to sell a piece, use this list. You will feel better about parting with a piece if the buyer is someone you know will enjoy it.

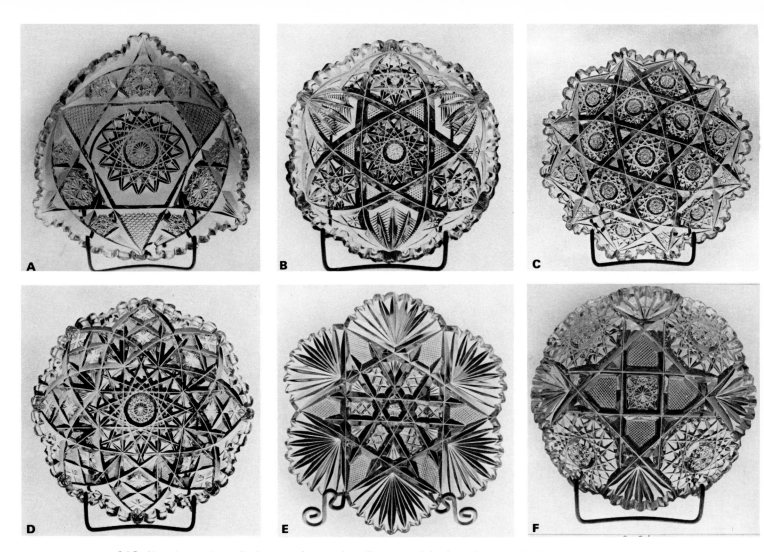

218. Nappies and small plates make good trading material when they can be bought at a modest price. **A.** Nappy that is eye-catching because of its shape. **B.** Nappy with 10-point hobstars and with fans done in a spiderweb motif. *Ardene Fairchild Smith.* **C.** A 6-inch plate with a cluster of hobstars, suggesting Hoare. **D.** Heavily cut nappy that resembles the work of Libbey. **E.** A 5-inch plate with fans dominating the pattern. *Patrick Curry.* **F.** A 5-inch nappy in hobstar and fan with a crosshatched base.

Cataloging a Collection

Every collector should keep a record of what he buys, receives, or inherits. Record sheets can be mimeographed very cheaply. The following format is the one we use:

NAME OF ITEM _____ NUMBER _____

DESCRIPTION _____

_____

SIGNATURE _____

PATTERN _____

CONDITION _____

COST OF REPAIRS _____

PRICE _____ DATE _____ VALUE _____

Some collectors use an electric needle to mark a number on a piece; others use a small paper sticker. Under "Condition," describe any chips, bruises, and the like. If you have a piece restored, state the cost of the work and describe exactly what was done (add the cost of repairs to the original price). "Date" refers to the date of purchase. Under "Value," indicate whether you feel the piece was underpriced, overpriced, or priced accurately (express this in dollars).

If possible, take a photograph of the item and attach it to the record sheet or card—a Polaroid picture will do. By all means keep the sales slip for each piece of glass and file it with the card. Update the value periodically according to what you observe at shows or learn from talking with collectors and visiting antiques shops. Use the back of the card or sheet to give the year of updating and the new dollar value. This record-keeping is one of the more important parts of collecting. It is a protection in the event of loss and useful for insurance purposes as well.

A number of insurance companies offer a fine arts policy that covers such things as damage from fire, breakage, and theft. The cost is nominal compared to other insurance. You can secure information on such a policy by getting in touch with any insurance agency. A homeowner's policy often does not cover the full value of a collection.

219. Some collectors concentrate on small items. **A.** An individual pedestal salt signed Libbey on the base. **B.** A pastepot and an individual salt. The pastepot (or mucilage bottle) is listed in the S. F. Myers catalog. *Rita Klyce.* **C.** A master pedestal salt.

172   Research on American cut glass never ends. With so many people interested in the subject, more and more old company records and catalogs are coming to light to expand present knowledge. The continual search for authenticity adds fascination and challenge to the hobby. There is always a chance that *any* collector, anywhere, may make some new discovery on his own (Ill. 220).

One fact remains unchanged and unchallenged: Brilliant cut glass is an irreplaceable part of our historical heritage. Americans made the finest cut glass in the world, so treasure your collection and enjoy its exquisite beauty.

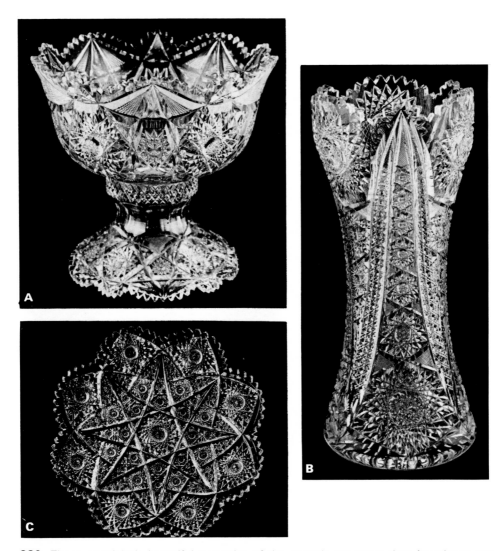

220. These exquisitely beautiful examples of the cutter's art prove that Americans cut the finest glass in the world: **A.** Punch bowl in Waverly pattern, signed Libbey, appeared in the 1900-1910 catalog. *Hunt Collection.* **B.** A 12-inch vase cut with chains of hobstars and beading. *Hunt Collection.* **C.** A 12-inch plate with a star consisting of radiating hobstars. *C. W. Moody*

Appendix

AMERICAN SIGNATURES

C. G. ALFORD & COMPANY
New York, New York

T. B. CLARK & COMPANY
Honesdale, Pennsylvania

T. G. HAWKES & COMPANY
Corning, New York

ALMY & THOMAS
Corning, New York

C. DORFLINGER & SONS
White Mills, Pennsylvania

J. HOARE & COMPANY
Corning, New York

M. J. AVERBECK MANUFACTURER
New York, New York

O. F. EGGINTON COMPANY
Corning, New York

HOBBS GLASS COMPANY
Wheeling, West Virginia

J. D. BERGEN COMPANY
Meriden, Connecticut

H. C. FRY GLASS COMPANY
Rochester, Pennsylvania

HOPE GLASS WORKS
Providence, Rhode Island

173

HUNT GLASS COMPANY
Corning, New York

IRVING CUT GLASS COMPANY
Honesdale, Pennsylvania

LACKAWANNA CUT GLASS COMPANY Scranton, Pennsylvania

LAUREL CUT GLASS COMPANY
Jermyn, Pennsylvania

LIBBEY GLASS COMPANY
Toledo, Ohio

LYONS CUT GLASS COMPANY
Lyons, New York

MAJESTIC CUT GLASS COMPANY
Elmira, New York

MAPLE CITY GLASS COMPANY
Hawley, Pennsylvania

NEWARK CUT GLASS COMPANY
Newark, New Jersey

PAIRPOINT CORPORATION
New Bedford, Massachusetts

P. X. PARSCHE & SON COMPANY
Chicago, Illinois

PITKIN & BROOKS
Chicago, Illinois

SIGNET GLASS COMPANY
Address unknown

H. P. SINCLAIRE & COMPANY
Corning, New York

STERLING GLASS COMPANY
Cincinnati, Ohio

L. STRAUS & SONS
New York, New York

TAYLOR BROTHERS
Philadelphia, Pennsylvania

TUTHILL CUT GLASS COMPANY
Middletown, New York

UNGER BROTHERS
Newark, New Jersey

VAN HEUSEN, CHARLES COMPAN
Albany, New York

WRIGHT RICH CUT GLASS COMPANY Anderson, Indiana

Unidentified American Signatures

CANADIAN SIGNATURES

HOUSE OF BIRKS

Montreal, Canada

GOWANS, KENT & COMPANY LIMITED

Toronto, Canada

GUNDY-CLAPPERTON COMPANY

Toronto, Canada

RODEN BROTHERS

Toronto, Canada

Unidentified Canadian Signature

INDEX OF ILLUSTRATED PATTERNS

Aberdeen	Hawkes	Ill. 76
Aberdeen	Jewel	Ill. 86
Adam	Sinclaire	Ill. 106
Alhambra (Greek Key)	Meriden	Ills. 30, 98
Apples, Grapes, and Pears	Sinclaire	Ill. 18
Arabian	Egginton	Ill. 73
Arabian Nights	Averbeck	Ill. 58
Arcadia	Sterling	Ill. 107
Athole	Pitkin & Brooks	Ills. 102, 103
Atlantic	Empire	Ill. 74
Avila	Pairpoint	Ill. 100
Azalia	Averbeck	Ill. 64
Baker's Gothic	Clark	Ill. 69
Baronial	Sinclaire	Ill. 105
Bedford	Bergen	Ills. 62, 65, 141
Belmont	Pitkin & Brooks	Ill. 103
Bengal	Sinclaire	Ill. 105
Bermuda	Bergen	Ill. 62
Border	Pitkin & Brooks	Ill. 104
Boston	Averbeck	Ill. 59
Bowa	Pitkin & Brooks	Ill. 102
Brazilian	Hawkes	Ill. 77
Brunswick	Hawkes	Ills. 75, 77, 78, 106
Calvé	Egginton	Ill. 5, 72
Canton	Averbeck	Ill. 57
Caprice	Bergen	Ill. 61
Cardinal	Hawkes	Ill. 76
Chrysanthemum	Hawkes	Ills. 1, 42, 75, 214
Claremont	Bergen	Ill. 64
Cleo	Pitkin & Brooks	Ill. 103
Cluster	Egginton	Ill. 72
Colombia	Blackmer	Ills. 66, 153
*"Corinthian"**	Clark	Ill. 67
*"Corinthian"**	Irving	Ill. 129

*Names in quotation marks represent common usage but are not listed in official catalogs.

Corinthian	Libbey	Ills. 88, 92, 145
Corinthian	Straus	Ill. 108
Corsair	Bergen	Ill. 62
Corsair	Pitkin & Brooks	Ill. 101
Cortez	Pitkin & Brooks	Ill. 102
Creswick	Egginton	Ill. 73
Creswick	Hoare	Ill. 82
Dallas	Bergen	Ill. 63
Dariel	Bergen	Ill. 61
Delphos	Libbey	Ill. 93
Devonshire	Hawkes	Ills. 69, 78, 155
Diamond	Averbeck	Ill. 57
Diamond and Silver Threads	Sinclaire	Ill. 166
Diamond Strawberry	Dorflinger	Ill. 70
Elaine	Bergen	Ill. 63
Electric	Bergen	Ill. 60
Elsmere	Libbey	Ill. 95
Emblem	Bergen	Ill. 61
Empress	Averbeck	Ill. 57
Empress	Libbey	Ill. 44
Empress	Quaker City Cut Glass Company	Ill. 166
Eulalia	Libbey	Ills. 88, 90
"Expanding Star"	unknown	Ills. 54, 210
Fancy Prism	Hawkes	Ill. 16
Festoon	Hawkes	Ills. 23, 79
Florence	Hoare	Ills. 83, 122, 200
Florence	Libbey	Ills. 91, 191
Flute		Ill. 48
Flute and Panel Border	Sinclaire	Ill. 105
Frisco	Averbeck	Ills. 57, 58
Frisco	Bergen	Ill. 62
Genoa	Averbeck	Ill. 60
Gladys	Hawkes	Ills. 79, 165
Glencoe	Hawkes	Ill. 77
Glenda	Libbey	Ill. 94
Glenwood	Bergen	Ill. 63
Gloria	Libbey	Ill. 93
Golf	Bergen	Ill. 62
Grapes	Sinclaire	Ill. 17
Gravic Iris	Hawkes	Ills. 80, 81
Grecian	Hawkes	Ill. 1
Harvard		Ills. 49, 52, 190, 192
Harvard	Libbey	Ills. 13, 95, 127
Hawthorne	Bergen	Ill. 61
Heart	Pitkin & Brooks	Ill. 103, 206
Hindoo	Hoare	Ills. 45, 82
Hobnail		Ill. 49
"Horseshoe" ("Good Luck")	Kupfer	Ill. 87
Imperial	Libbey	Ills. 88, 89
"Intaglio Fruit"	Tuthill	Ill. 133
Inverness	Dorflinger	Ill. 71
Iola	Libbey	Ill. 95

177

178	*Iowa*	Irving	Ill. 85
	Jewel	Libbey	Ill. 90
	Kenwood	Bergen	Ill. 62
	Keystone	Bergen	Ill. 61
	Key West	Bergen	Ill. 61
	Kingston	Libbey	Ill. 92
	Lady Curzon	Averbeck	Ill. 57
	Lakefield	Lakefield (Canada)	Ill. 161
	Laurel	Bergen	Ill. 61
	Libbey	Libbey	Ill. 92
	Liberty	Averbeck	Ills. 57, 60
	Logan	Bergen	Ill. 64
	Lotus	Egginton	Ills. 72, 73
	Magnet	Bergen	Ills. 61, 62
	Marcella	Libbey	Ill. 88
	Marietta	Averbeck	Ill. 57
	Meadville	Pitkin & Brooks	Ill. 101
	Middlesex	Dorflinger	Ill. 69
	Middlesex	Hawkes	Ills. 77, 190
	Mikado	Pitkin & Brooks	Ill. 101
	Monarch	Hoare	Ills. 82, 155
	Morgan	Unknown	Ill. 7
	Myrtle	Pitkin & Brooks	Ills. 101, 104
	Nassau	Hoare	Ills. 82, 83, 189
	Nautilus	Hawkes	Ill. 76
	Navarre	Hawkes	Ill. 81
	Nellore	Pitkin & Brooks	Ill. 102
	Nelson	Empire	Ill. 74
	Nelson	Hawkes	Ill. 175
	New Brilliant	Libbey	Ill. 95
	Notched Prism		Ills. 47, 140
	Notched Prism	Bergen	Ill. 64
	Notched Prism	Fry	Ill. 190
	No. 80	Dorflinger	Ill. 70
	No. 100	Libbey	Ill. 93
	No. 136	Meriden	Ill. 97
	No. 227F	Meriden	Ill. 96
	No. 1023	Sinclaire	Ill. 40
	No. 72016	Marshall Field Catalog	Ill. 46
	Occident	Averbeck	Ill. 58
	Osborn	Pitkin & Brooks	Ill. 103
	Ozella	Libbey	Ill. 92
	"Palm Leaf Fan"	Ohio	Ill. 99
	Panel	Hawkes	Ill. 79
	"Panel & Flute"		Ill. 48
	Paola	Dorflinger	Ills. 70, 126
	Paris	Averbeck	Ill. 58
	Parisian	Dorflinger	Ills. 70, 71
	Pilgrim	Bergen	Ill. 61
	Pinwheel	Clark	Ill. 68
	Prima Donna	Clark	Ill. 68
	Princess	Libbey	Ill. 89
	Princess	O'Connor	Ill. 99
	Priscilla	Averbeck	Ill. 57
	Prism	Averbeck	Ill. 59

Prism	Libbey	Ill. 94
Progress	Bergen	Ill. 62
Puck	Averbeck	Ill. 58
Puritana	Libbey	Ill. 88
Plymouth	Meriden	Ills. 97, 98
Plymouth	Pitkin & Brooks	Ill. 103
Queens	Hawkes	Ill. 80
Queens	Hoare	Ill. 83
Queens	Sinclaire	Ill. 105
Radiant	Mt. Washington	Ills. 99, 150
Rajah	Libbey	Ill. 92
Rajah	Pitkin & Brooks	Ill. 104
Ripple	Bergen	Ill. 61
Roland	Pitkin & Brooks	Ill. 102
Royal	Averbeck	Ill. 57
Royal	Hunt	Ills. 53, 84, 210
Ruby	Averbeck	Ill. 57
Russian	Corning	Ill. 192
Russian	Hawkes	Ill. 170
Russian	Pairpoint	Ills. 4, 100
Russian Canterbury		Ills. 12, 53
Russian Cleveland		Ill. 53
Russian Persian		Ills. 4, 53
Russian Polar Star		Ill. 53
Rye	Bergen (R.T. & Co. Jewelers)	Ill. 46
Saratoga	Averbeck	Ills. 57, 58
Satin Chrysanthemum	Hawkes	Ill. 110
Senora	Libbey	Ill. 91
Silver Thread	Libbey	Ill. 86
Spillane	Libbey	Ill. 92
Spruce	Averbeck	Ills. 58, 59
Star	Pitkin & Brooks	Ill. 102
Star and Feather	Libbey	Ill. 93
Strawberry Diamond		Ill. 26
Strawberry-Diamond and Fan		Ills. 26, 49, 50
Strawberry-Diamond and Star	Clark	Ill. 68
Sultana	Blackmer	Ill. 66
Sultana	Libbey	Ill. 89
Sunburst		Ill. 55
Sunset	Libbey	Ill. 91
"Thistle"	unknown	Ill. 170
"Three Fruits"	Hawkes	Ill. 18
"Tulip"	Mt. Washington	Ill. 99
Venetian	Hawkes	Ills. 75, 76
Victrola	Irving	Ill. 85
Viscaria	Pairpoint	Ill. 15
Wabash	Bergen	Ill. 63
Waverly	Libbey	Ills. 90, 220
Webster	Higgins & Seiter Catalog	Ill. 22
Webster	Bergen	Ill. 62
Wedgemere	Libbey	Ill. 88
Westminister	Sinclaire	Ill. 106
Wheat	Hoare	Ill. 150
Wheeler	Mt. Washington	Ill. 98
Wild Rose	Tuthill	Ill. 110

Index

Note: page numbers in *italics* refer to illustrations

Abbott, George L., 61
Aberdeen pattern, 57, *58,* 63, *63*
Acid bath (acid polishing), 13, 136, 138, 151, 165
Adam pattern, 78, *79*
Adapted pieces, 116
Adelaide pattern, 74
Age marks, 111
Albert Steffin pattern, 73
Alford, C. G., & Company, 45, 173
Alford signature, 103
Alhambra pattern, 71, *72*
Almy, Charles H., 45
Almy & Thomas, 45, 66, 94, 103, 173
Ambassador pattern, 42
American Cut Glass Company, 33, 74
Anderson, William C., 65, 68
Annealing, 9
Antique shows and shops, 150, 157, 166
    See also Flea markets; Garage sales
Antiques magazines (antiques tabloids), 151, 157, 164, 166
Apples, Grapes, and Pears pattern, *18,* 78
Appraisal, *see* Evaluating cut glass
Arabian pattern, 54, *55,* 136
Arcadia pattern, 80, *80*
Aster pattern, 78
Athole pattern, 75, *76*
Atlantic pattern, 56, *56*
Auctions, 150-51, 157
Averbeck Cut Glass Company (M. J. Averbeck Manufacturer), 46-47, 50, 66, 94, 103
Avila pattern, 74, *74*
Azalia pattern, *50*

Baker, Thomas A., 53
Barnes, James B., 61
Baronial pattern, 78, *79*
Bases, 111, 139, *140,* 141, *141, 142*
Bashford, James, 69
Baskets, handles on, 108, 142
Baumann, Harry, 84
Beading motif, *5,* 22, *23*
Bedford pattern, *50,* 107
Belleville Cut Glass Company, 125
Belmont pattern, 75, *76*
Bengal pattern, 78, *79*
Bergen, James D., 48
Bergen, J. D., Company, 30, 33, 39, 40, 47-50
    signatures of, *173*
Bergen Cut Glass Company, 14, 15, 50, 107, 145, 155
    signatures, 94, 101
Bergen pattern, *50*

Birks, *see* House of Birks
Blackmer, Arthur L., 51
Blackmer Cut Glass Company, 51, 119
Blakewell, B., & Company, 4
Blanks, *see* Glass blanks
Blaze motif, 20, *20*
Block motif, 24
Block pattern, 41
Bohemian glass makers, 7-8, 133
Border pattern, 75, *78*
Boston pattern, 47
Bottles and decanters, *40, 41, 47, 72, 79,* 98, 101, *141, 161*
    necks on, 143
    See also Stoppers
Bowa pattern, *76*
Bowls, *21, 87, 99, 131, 134, 135*
    banana, *138*
    berry, *112,* 122, *124,* 132
    rose, *117*
    signature placement on, 98, 101
Boxes, signature placement on, 98
    with silver fittings, 16, *17, 61*
Brazilian pattern, 3, 57, *58*
Bread trays, 122, *158*
Brilliant Period (1876-1906), 3-6, 22, 24, 25, 136, 146
Brooklyn Flint Glass Company, 60
Brooks, Jonathan William, 75
Bruises, 111, *112,* 164
Brunswick pattern, 57, *57, 59, 79*
Butter dish, covered, *58, 71, 97, 119,* 122, *169*
    open, *61*
Butter pats, 98, 122
Buying cut glass, 109-28, 153, 155, 157, 161
    adapted pieces, 116
    colored, 128
    damaged pieces, 109-15
    foreign pieces, 123-26
    mismated pieces, 118-19, *118-21*
    modern pieces, *126,* 127, *127*
    repaired pieces, 115-16, *117*
    wrong identification in, 121-23
        See also Antique shows and shops; Estate sales; Evaluating cut glass; Flea markets
Buzz motif, 33, *33*

Calvé pattern, *5,* 32, 54, *55*
Canadian glass, 94, 123-26, 133
    signatures on, *175*
Cane pattern, 26, 42, 141
Canterbury pattern, 42, *43, 130*
Carborundum wheels, 12
Carder, Frederick, 57

Cardinal pattern, 57, *58*
Care of glass, 162-63
    See also Repairs
Cassidy Limited, 123
Cataloging a collection, 170-71
Celery trays, *53, 92,* 122, *160*
Centennial Exposition (1876, Philadelphia), 1
Chips, 110, *110,* 164, 165
Chrysanthemum pattern, 2, *2,* 37, 57, *57, 87,* 91, 145, *167*
    See also Satin Chrysanthemum pattern
Clapperton, H. G., 123
Claremont pattern, *50*
Clark, Thomas Byron, 51
Clark, T. B., & Company, 3, 15, 22, 28, 33, 40, 51-53, 121, 132, 160, 164
    signature of, 86, 87, 89, 91, 92, 94-99, 101, 102, 104, 108, *173*
Cleaning, *see* Polishing; Washing
Cleo pattern, 75, *77*
Cleveland, Grover, 42
Cleveland pattern, 42, *43*
Cloudiness, 115, 165
Cluster pattern, 54, *55*
Collection
    cataloging a, 170-71
    displaying a, 163, 166
    upgrading a, 169
        See also specific topics
Colombia pattern, 51, *51,* 119
Colored cut glass, 128, 145, 151
Colored-cut-to-clear glass, 14-15
Colored overlay glass, 9
Comparative pricing, 150-52
Copper wheel cutting, 17, 34-35
Cordova, Julian de, 82
Corinthian pattern, 36, 51, *51,* 63, 65, *65,* 67, 80, *81, 112,* 136, 164
Corning Flint Glass Company, 60
Corning Glass Works, 45, 54, 57, 63, 147
Corning Museum, 166
Coronal pattern, 74
Corsair pattern, *75*
Cortez pattern, *76*
Covered (lidded) dishes, 145, *147*
Cracks, 111, *112,* 113-14, 165
Creswick pattern, 54, *55,* 60, *60, 159*
Crosshatching motif, *25,* 26, *27*
Crystal Wash, 162
Curved miter, 20, *21*
Cut Glass Corporation of America, 64, 78
Cutting, evaluation of, 136-39
Cutting wheels, 10, 12
    copper, 34-35

Daisy motif, 6
Dallas pattern, *49*
Damaged pieces, 109-15, 164, 165
Decanters, *see* Bottles and decanters
De Goey, John R., 61
De Goey, W. Edmund, 61
Delphos pattern, 65, *68*
Design, quality in, 134, *135*
 See also Patterns
Devonshire pattern, *53,* 57, *59,* 120
Diamond motif, 24, *25,* 130
Diamond-Strawberry pattern, 53, *54*
Diaz, Porfirio, 3, 58
Dingwall, 124
Displaying a collection, 163, 166
Dobelmann, J. D., 1
Dorflinger, C., & Sons, 1, 3, 4, 10, 20, 28, 30,
 40, 43, 53-54, 78, 95, 103-4, 113
 signature of, 103, 105, *173*
Dorflinger, Christian, 1, 2, 51, 53, 88, 166
Dorflinger, William, 2

Early Period (1830-1876), 4
Edward VIII, King of England, 3
Egginton, O. F., Company, 54-55, 123, 160, 164
 signature of, 86, 91, 101, 105, *173*
Egginton, Oliver F., 3, 32, 54, 88, 94
Elaine pattern, *49*
Electric pattern, *47*
Elsmere pattern, 65, *69*
Empire Cut Glass Company, 56
Empress pattern, *37,* 65, 78, *130*
English glass, 7, 26, 133
Engraving, 4, 17, 78
 copper wheel, 34
Estate sales, 157
Etching, 4
Eulalia pattern, 65, *65,* 66
Evaluating cut glass, 129-52
 comparative pricing, 150-52
 quality, 129. *See also* Standards of quality
Ewer, N. J., & Sons, 69
Expanding Star pattern, 44, *44, 162*

Fancy Prism pattern, *18,* 57
Fan motif, 14, 22, *23, 25*
Festoon pattern, 57, *59*
Figured blank, 6
Flakes, 110, *111,* 164
Flashed star motif, 32, *32*
Flat star motif, 30, *30*
Flea markets, 153, 155
Flemington Cut Glass Company, 56
Florence pattern, 32, 60, *61,* 65, *67, 93, 147, 155*
Flower motifs, 34-35, *35*
Flower Period (1906-1916), 3, 6, 7, 136, 145
Flute and Panel Border pattern, 78, *79*
Flute motif, 28, *29*
Flute pattern, *40*
Foreign glass, 123-26
 See also Bohemian glass makers; Canadian
  glass; English glass; Irish glass
Forged signatures, 108
Foster and Bailey, 105
Fractures, 111, 165
Fringe motif, 20, *20*
Fruit motifs, 34-35, *35*
Fry, H. C., Glass Company, 6, 7, 15, 30, 34, 56,
 63, 77, 131, 146, 166, 168
 signatures of, 92, 93, 96, 98, 100, 101, *173*

Garage sales, 155
Genoa pattern, *47*
Geometric motifs, 24-34
 block, 24
 buzz, 33, *33*
 crosshatching, *25,* 26, *27*
 diamond, 24, *25,* 130
 flute, 28, *29*
 hobnail, 26, *26*
 key, 27, *27*

star, 28-33, *29-33*
 thumbprint, 28, *28*
German Cut Glass Company, 64
Gerould, Otis, 9, 11, *12,* 13, *13,* 115
Gilliland, John L., & Company, 4
Gillinder, William, 2
Gillinder & Sons, 1
Gladys pattern, 57, *59, 90*
Glass
 ingredients of, 7-8
 scissile, 115
 sick, 115, 165
Glass blanks, 131-33
 evaluating cut glass and, 136, *138*
 figured, 6
 making, 7-9
Glencoe pattern, 57, *58*
Glenda pattern, 65, *68*
Glenwood pattern, *49*
Gloria pattern, 65, *68*
"Good Luck" pattern, 64, *64*
Gorham Corporation, 105, 106
Gothic pattern, 51, *53*
Gould & Hoare, 60
Gowans, Kent & Company, Limited, 123, 124,
 175
Grapes pattern, *18*
Gravic Chrysanthemum pattern, 57
Gravic glass, 17, 35
Gravic Iris pattern, 57
Grecian pattern, 2, *2,* 57
Greek key motif, 27, *27*
Greek Key pattern, 71
Gundy-Clapperton Company, 59, 123, 124, 175

Handles, 142, *142,* 143, *143,* 151
 heat checks and, 114
 signature placement, in relation to, 98, 101
Harrison, Benjamin, 42
Harvard pattern, 14, *15,* 26, *26,* 42, *42, 43,* 51,
 51, 65, *69, 97, 112, 138,* 141, *141,* 143, *146,*
 147, 158
Hatch, George E., 65
Hawken, William H., 63
Hawkes, Samuel, 57
Hawkes, T. G., & Company, 9, 10, 15, 28, 32,
 34, 35, 37, 40, 42, 43, 53, 55, 57-60, 65, 66,
 79, 82, 113, 120, 121, 130-32, 137, 143,
 144-47, 149, 154, 166, 167
 signature of, 86, 89-91, 94, 98-101, 105, 108,
 173
Hawkes, Thomas Gibbon, 2, 34, 43, 57, 88, 93,
 94
 intaglio cutting by, 17, *18*
Hawkes, Townsend de M., 57
Hawkes Gravic Glass, 17, 18
Healy, Patrick H., 33
Heart pattern, 75, *77, 159*
Heat checks, 114
Higgins & Seiter, 22, 38-39, 123, 145
Hindoo pattern, *38,* 60, *60*
Hoare, J., & Company, 2, 4, 6, 21, 23, 30, 32
 59-61, 95, 110, 114, 117, 120, 144, 155,
 159, 161, 166
 signature of, 86-89, 91, 93, 94, 97, 98, 100-
 102, 104, *173*
Hoare, John, 60, 93
Hoare & Burns, 60
Hobbs, Brockunier Company, 1
Hobbs, John L., 61
Hobbs Glass Company, 61, *173*
Hobbs Gold Medal (signature), 103
Hobnail motif, 26, *26*
Hobnail pattern, 41
Hobstar motif, 30, *30,* 31, 134
Hollis, Harry, 56
Honeycomb pattern, 40
Hope Glass Works, 61-62, 103, *173*
"Horseshoe" pattern, *64*
Houghton, Amory, 82
House of Birks, 61, 125, 175
Howe, Timothy, 73

Hunt, Harry, 63
Hunt, Thomas, 63
Hunt Glass Company, 62, 63, 103, 144, 162, 174

Ice cream trays and plates, 88, *95,* 122, *138, 139*
Identification
 by label, 103-4
 on liner, 106-7
 by motif, 19
 by pattern, 36-39
 by signature, *see* Signatures
 of silver parts, 105-6. *See also* Silver decoration
 wrong, 121-23
Imperial pattern, *55,* 65, *65, 66,* 136
Insurance, 171
Intaglio cutting, 17, *18,* 34-35, 77, 82, 145, *146,*
 151
Intaglio Iris pattern, 57
International Silver Company, 71, 105
Inverness pattern, 53, *54*
Iola pattern, 65, *69*
Iowa pattern, *62,* 63
Iris pattern, *59, 60*
Irish glass, 7-8, 133
Irving Cut Glass Company, Inc., 34, 51, 62, 63,
 144
 signature of, 87, 98, 99, 108, *174*

Jarves, Deming, 73
Jewel Cut Glass Company, 63
Jewel pattern, 65, *66,* 93

Kern, Martin L., 61
Key motif, 27, *27*
Key pattern, 71
Kingston pattern, 65, *67*
Knickerbocker Cut Glass Company, 45
Knife rests, 101, 122
Kotwitz, Frank, 84
Kotwitz, Herman, 84
Krantz, John E., 64
Krantz-Smith & Company, 63, 64
Kupfer, Emil F., Inc., 64

Labels, 103-4
Lackawanna Cut Glass Company, 64, 103, 174
Lakefield Cut Glass Company, 125, 126
Lakefield pattern, *126*
Lalonde, Joe, 18
Lamps, 101, 145, *146*
Landenwitsch, Joseph, 80
Lattice pattern, 136
Laurel Cut Glass Company, 62, 64, 78, 174
Lead, 7, 8
Lehr, 9
Libbey, Edward Drummond, 65
Libbey, Capt. Henry, 73
Libbey, William L., 38, 65, 73
Libbey Glass Company, 1, 2, 15, 18, 28, 30, 34-
 37, 51, 63, 65-70, 97, 112, 114, 130, 131,
 143, 144, 147, 161, 164, 166, 171, 172
 signatures of, 89-91, 93, 94, 97-102, *174*
Libbey pattern, 65, *67*
Liberty pattern, *47*
Lincoln pattern, 74
Line motifs, 20-23
Liners, 106, *107,* 145
Logan pattern, *50*
Long Island Flint Glass Works, 53
Lotus pattern, 54, *55*
Lozenges, 22, *25*
Luckock, Henry L., 63
Luster, 131, *131, 138*
Lyons Cut Glass Company, 69, 174

McD Brothers (unidentified signature), 103,
 104, *175*
McDonald, Phillip, 10, 42, 103
McKinley, William, 42
Majestic Cut Glass Company, 70
 signature of, 103, *174*

Maple City Glass Company, 24, 70
  signature of, 90, 94, *174*
Marcella pattern, *65*
Marrett, William, 63, 65, 68
Marshall Field & Company, 84, 145
Matched sets, appraisal of, 145
Matching pieces, 166, 168
  See also Mismated pieces
Meadville pattern, *75*
Menocal, Mario, 3
Meriden Cut Glass Company, 27, 32, 70-72
  signature of, 105
Meriden Silver Plate Company, 71
Middlesex pattern, 53, *53,* 57, *58,* 136, *146*
Mikado pattern, *75*
Miniatures, 121, 145, *147*
Mismated pieces, 118-19, *118-21*
Mitchell (unidentified signature), 97, 103, *175*
Miter motif, 20, *21*
Modern cut glass, *126,* 127, *127,* 133
Monarch pattern, 39, 60, *60,* 120
Monroe, C. F., Company, 105
Morgan pattern, *7*
Motifs
  beading, 22, *23*
  blaze or fringe, 20, *20*
  buzz, 33, *33*
  evaluating cut glass and, 134-37
  fan, 14, 22, *23*
  flower, 34-35, *35*
  flute, 28, *29*
  geometric, *see* Geometric motifs
  identification by, 19
  key, 27, *27*
  line, 20-23
  minor, 134, *135,* 136, *137*
  miter, 20, *21*
  pinwheel, 28, 33, 51, *52*
  star, *5,* 28-33, *29-33*
  step, 20, *21*
  thumbprint, 28, *28*
Mount Washington Glass Company, 1, 14, 32,
  34, 71-74, 117
Murray, Lot, 50
Myers, S. F., catalog, 171
Myrtle pattern, 75, *75, 78*

NACGMO (unidentified signature), 124, 125,
  175
Nailhead diamond motif, 24, *25*
Napkin rings, 101, 122
Napoleon pattern, 39
Nappies
  handles on, 142-43
  identification of, 122
Nassau pattern, 60, *60, 61,* 144
National Association of Dealers in Antiques, Inc.,
  157
Nautilus pattern, 57, *58*
Navarre pattern, 57, *60*
Nellore pattern, *76*
Nelson pattern, 56, *56,* 57, *137*
Newark Cut Glass Company, signature of, *174*
New Brilliant pattern, 65, *69*
New England Glass Company, 1, 43
Niland, Thomas A., 48
Notched prism pattern, 39, *40, 50, 143, 146, 159*
Novelties, 145, *147, 149*
No. 80 pattern, 53, *54*
No. 100 pattern, 65, *68*
No. 136 pattern, *70,* 71
No. 227 pattern, 71, *71*

O'Connor, Arthur E., 74
O'Connor, J. S., 10, 20, 70, 73, 74, 88
Ohio Cut Glass Company, 74
Osborn pattern, 75, *77*
Oskamp, Nolting Company, 145
Ottawa Cut Glass Company, 125
Overlay glass, 9
Ozella pattern, 65, *67*

Pairpoint Manufacturing Company, 1, 15, 41,
  43, 50, 73, 74, 106, 118
  signature of, 105, *174*
Palm Leaf pattern, 74
Panel pattern, *40,* 57, *59*
Paola pattern, 53, *54, 95*
Paris Exposition (1889), 2
Parisian pattern, 10, 14, 53, *54,* 136
Parsche, P. X., & Son Company, 174
Patents, 87-89
Patterns (designs), 10, 12
  definition of, 19
  descriptive name, 44
  evaluating cut glass and, 134-36
  identification by, 36-39
  public domain, 39-43
    See also specific patterns
Pedestal (pedestal pieces), 139, *140,* 141, *141,*
  142
  foot of, 116
  signature placement on, 101
Persian pattern, 42
Persian variation of Russian pattern, *5*
Philadelphia, 1876 Centennial Exposition in, 1
Phillips, George, & Company, 124
Phillips, Joseph, 80
Pineapple diamond motif, 24
Pinwheel motif, 28, 33, 51, *52*
Pitchers
  signature placement on, 98, 101
  weight of, 132
Pitkin, Edward Hand, 75
Pitkin and Brooks Company, 10, 11, 75-78, 95,
  131, 144, 148, 159
  signature of, 86, 101, *174*
Place setting, Victorian, 121-22
Plates
  identification of, 122
  signature placement on, 98
Plymouth pattern, 71, *71, 72,* 75, *77*
Pointed diamond motif, 24
Polar Star Russian pattern, 42-43, *43*
Polishing, 13, 136, 138, 151, 164, 165
Porte & Markle, 125, 175
Price guides, annual, 150
Prices, 129, 139, 157
Pricing, comparative, 150-52
Prima Donna pattern, 51, *52*
Primrose pattern, 77
Princess pattern, 65, *66, 73,* 74
Prism pattern, 65, *68*
  See also Notched prism pattern
Public domain patterns, 39-43
Puritana pattern, *65*
Pyramidal star motif, 30

Quaker City Cut Glass Company, 64, 78, 130
Quality, 129
  See also Standards of quality
Queens pattern, 57, *59,* 60, *61,* 78, *79*
Quinte-Clapperton Amalgamated, 123

Radiant pattern, 73, *73, 117*
Rainbow, 145
Rajah pattern, 65, *67,* 75, *78*
Rarity, 145-49, 151
Relief diamond motif, 24, *25*
Relish dishes, *155*
  identification of, 122
  signature placement on, 98
Repaired pieces, buying, 115-16, *117*
Repairs, 164-65
Replating of silver fittings, 113, 165
Rhythmic cutting, 3
Richardson, Solon O., Jr., 65
Riedal Glass Company, 8, 9, 12
Rims
  repairing, 116
  sawtooth, 116
  silver, 113, 114, *114*
Ring, 133-34

Rochester Tumbler Company, 56
"Rock crystal," 17, *18*
Roden Brothers, 124-26, 175
Rogers Brothers, 105
Roland pattern, *76*
Roman key motif, 27
Roosevelt, Franklin D., 42
Roosevelt, Theodore, 42
Rosette motif, 32
Roughness versus sharpness, 136
Royal pattern, 43, *62,* 63, 144, *162*
R. T. & Company Jewelers, 39
Russian Ambassador pattern, *43*
Russian Canterbury pattern, 42, *43, 130*
Russian Cleveland pattern, 42, *43*
Russian pattern, 4, *5,* 10, 26, 30, *51,* 74, *74,* 103,
  118, 141, *147*
  on colored cut glass, 14, *14*
Russian Persian pattern, 42, *43*
Rye pattern, *39*

St. Lawrence Glass Company, 123
St. Louis diamond motif, *23,* 24, *140,* 143
Salts, 121-22
Satin Chrysanthemum pattern, 57, *82*
Sawtooth rims, 116
Scarcity, 151
Schosger, Frank, 147
Scissile glass, 115
Scratches, 111
Sediment, removal of, 163
Sell, George W., & Company, 64
Senora pattern, 65, *67*
Shaley, Thomas A., 71
Shape, unusual, 143, *143, 154, 155*
Sharpness, 136, 138, *138*
Shooting star motif, 30
Shotten Cut Glass Company, 107
Shreve and Company, 54, 90, 106, 107, 149
Sick glass, 115, 165
Signatures, 84-108, 151, 173-75
  appraisal and, 144
  of Canadian companies, *175*
  confusions, 93-95
  forged, 108
  history of, 85-95
  pieces without, 89-92
  placement of, 96-102
  unidentified, 103, *175*
    See also McD Brothers; Mitchell; NACGMO
Signet Glass Company, signature of, *174*
Silver decoration (silver fittings), 16-17, 145
  cracks covered by, 113, *113,* 114, *114*
  identification on, *61,* 90, 105-106, *107*
  removing and replacing, 165
  replating, 113, 165
Silver thread pattern, *63,* 65, *130*
Sinclaire, H. P., & Company, 10, 27, 32, 78-79,
  130, 151
  Apples, Grapes, and Pears pattern, *18*
  Grapes pattern, *18*
  signature of, 86, 87, 89, 98, 101, 105, *174*
Singleton, J. F., 123
Singleton, Thomas, 71, 73, 74, 88
Smith, Francis R., 64
Smith, John H., 64
Smith Brothers, 41
Spawling & Company, Chelsea Works, 151
Spiegel, Saul, 70
Spiegel, Wolf M., 70
Spillane, Dennis F., 65, 67
Spillane pattern, 65, *67*
Spooners, 22
  signature placement on, 98, 101
Standards of quality, 131-49
  cutting, 136-39
  glass blank, 131-33, 136, 138
  motif, 134-37
  pattern, 134-36
  unique features, 139-49
Star & Feathers pattern, 65, *68*

Star motif, *5*, 28-33, *29-33*
Star pattern, *76*
    See also Expanding Star pattern
Steffin, Albert, 73
Stemware, 139
    repaired, 116
Step motif, 20, *21*
Sterling Cut Glass Company, 80, 103, 162, 174
Steuben Glass Works, 57
Stoppers, 119, *120, 121, 133, 140, 141*
Straus, L., & Company, 30, 36, 51, 55, 80-81, 95
    signature of, *94*, 98, 100, *174*
Straus, Lazarus, 80
    See also Straus, L., & Company
Strawberry-Diamond and Fan pattern, 41, 57
Strawberry-Diamond and Star pattern, 51, *52*
Strawberry-diamond motif, 5, 24, *25*, 26
Strawberry-Diamond pattern, 14, 141, *142*, 143,
    144, 159
Sultana pattern, 51, *51*, 65, *66*
Sunburst pattern, 44
Sunset pattern, 65, *67*

Taylor, Albert, 80
Taylor, C. H., Glass Company, 63
Taylor, Lafayette, 80
Taylor Brothers, 80, 81
    signature of, *93*, 101, *174*
Thickness, of glass blank, 132, *132*, 133, 136,
    138
Thistle pattern, *133*
Thomas, G. Edwin, 45

Thomas Singleton pattern, 73
Three Fruits pattern, *18*
Thumbprint motif, 28, *28*
Tiffany & Company, Inc., 106, 107
Toledo Museum of Art, 145, 166
Trays
    identification of, 121, 122
    signature placement on, 98
Triple square pattern, *see* Prima Donna pattern
"Tulip" pattern, *73*
Tumblers, 132-33
    signature placement on, 101
Tuthill, Charles G., 77, 88, 89
Tuthill, James F., 77
Tuthill, Susan, 77
Tuthill Cut Glass Company, 20, 34-35, 77, 82,
    95, 144, 146
    signature of, *90*, *91*, 94, 97-102, *174*

Unger Brothers, 81, 82, 144, 174
Union Glass Company, 63, 69, 82, 83, 97, 106,
    107
Unique features, 139-49
    rarity, 145-49
    signatures, 144
    variation in form, 139-44
Upgrading a collection, 169

Van Heusen, Charles Company, 81, 84, 94, 174
Venetian glass makers, 8
Venetian pattern, 57, *57, 58*
Vesica, 20, 22, *25*

Victorian place setting, 121-22
Victrola pattern, *62*, 63
Viscaria pattern, *17*, 74

Wabash pattern, *49*
Wallace, R., & Son Manufacturing Company,
    105, 107
Wallaceburg Cut Glass Company, 123
Washing cut glass, 162-63
Watson Brothers, 124, 125
Waverly pattern, *66, 172*
Wear marks, 111
Webster pattern, 22
Weight, as quality criterion, 132-33
Western Cut Glass Company, 83, 84
Westminster pattern, 78, *79*
Wheat pattern, 60, *117*
Wheeler pattern, 14, *72*, 73
Wilcox, 17, 105
Wild Rose pattern, 77, *82*
Williams, John H., 80
Wisteria pattern, 35
Wixson, William L., 11, *11*, 12, *12*, 38, 39, 87,
    88
Wolstenholme, Thomas, 78
Wood, Walter A., 52, 94
World's Columbian Exposition (1893,
    Chicago), 2
Wright, George W., 84
Wright, Thomas W., 84
Wright Rich Cut Glass Company, 83, 84
    signature of, 101, 103, *174*